GOOD NEWS IN
ACTS

The *Acts of the Apostles*
in Today's English Version

Introduced by
DAVID L. EDWARDS

Collins
FONTANA BOOKS
In co-operation with The Bible Reading Fellowship

First published in Fontana Books 1975
Second Impression March 1975
© David L. Edwards 1975

Today's English Version of *The Acts of the Apostles*
© American Bible Society, New York, 1966, 1971

Made and printed in Great Britain by
William Collins Sons & Co Ltd Glasgow

CONDITIONS OF SALE

This book is sold subject to the condition
that it shall not, by way of trade or otherwise,
be lent, re-sold, hired out or otherwise circulated
without the publisher's prior consent in any form of
binding or cover other than that in which it is
published and without a similar condition
including this condition being imposed
on the subsequent purchaser

CONTENTS

PREFACE

Some of the books about *The Acts of the Apostles* are really sermons. They aim to improve the reader, but do not deal with questions about historical truth. Others are very different. They discuss the historical questions in detail, but do not help us to appreciate *Acts* as a powerful part of the Christian Bible. My introduction to this edition of *Acts* is one of the attempts which have been made to consider both historical and spiritual truth at the same time.

I say 'one of' such attempts – for there have been others, and I am indebted to them. But this attempt is special because it is based on Today's English Version for readers without much knowledge of the background – and also because it gets away from the custom of a sentence-by-sentence commentary. That method is appropriate to most parts of the Bible, but I believe that in the case of *Acts* what is most needed is something different: an effort to see the book as a whole, while not neglecting the details, which are often fascinating.

Among the many commentaries I have consulted, I mention only two. The first is *The Acts of the Apostles* by Dr William Neil of the University of Nottingham (1973). It defends the 'general historical reliability' of *Acts* and therefore may be labelled 'conservative'. It is brilliantly concise and it is convenient, for example in its up-to-date list of books for further reading. The other is *The Acts of the Apostles* by Professor Ernst Haenchen, translated into English from the fourteenth German edition in 1971. This standard work of over 700 pages, the fruit of the labour of twenty years, sums up, and adds to, the advanced studies of *Acts* in many languages. It may be labelled 'radical' because, generally speaking, it does not consider *Acts* to be accurate history.

D. L. E.

1. WE SHALL OVERCOME

In *The Acts of the Apostles* people who are really human – most of them heavily involved in the work of a city or a home – come to believe that a great new power is sweeping through their lives. But they do not believe that 'we shall overcome some day' in the distant future. For them, the day has arrived, and because of this every obstacle that remains can be overcome. They are deeply happy, and courageous, because they are like people who have heard the news of a victory. The war still goes on, but the main thing to do now is to get out in the streets and cheer.

Because it is a story of victory and celebration despite continuing struggles, *Acts* is to many readers the most enjoyable book in the Bible. (The gospels are too disturbing to be called enjoyable!) This may be difficult to believe, because *Acts* has so often been taught in schools as 'the journeys of St Paul'. So taught, it may become a complicated lesson in ancient geography, and a burden on the memory. But when read for its own sake *Acts* is a story full of interest, told by a master story-teller.

One is attracted by the physical adventure. This book is sun-soaked, spray-drenched, blood-stained. Christianity is launched like a great rocket despite riots, prisons, storms, and long roads. These Christians are like people who dance in the streets – and they also know how to fight their enemies (non-violently!). But one is more deeply impressed by the courage which these people show in accepting change. They sometimes act like people who can scarcely believe the good news – but they do believe it, and they are eager to share it.

The years covered are (very roughly speaking) AD 30 to AD 60. Within these years Christianity ceases to be a belief held by a few Jews in Palestine. It becomes (at least in principle) global: the world-religion which is to be the chief foundation of Europe, which is to be spread across the Atlantic and wherever Europeans go, which is to make a very substantial impact on Asia and Africa,

which is to become the most influential spiritual movement in the whole course of mankind's history. All this
involves an astonishing enlargement of the Christian
mind. When these people take the road from Jerusalem
to Rome, they accept not only physical dangers but also
the need to rethink – which is much harder.

One great attraction about *Acts* is that the journey of the
mind is told just as vividly as the journey of the body.
Modern psychology has made us familiar with the idea of
journeying *inwards* – to explore the depths hidden
beneath the surface of consciousness. Psychology has also
helped us to understand how these depths can appear in
our dream-life, when everyday habits and arguments can
be broken through to reveal what we are really feeling.

In chapter 10 of *Acts*, a fisherman is on the flat roof
of a house by the sea-front in the port of Joppa (now
Jaffa in Israel). He has gone there in order to find privacy
for meditation and prayer. He has a lot on his mind. He
is a Jew, and the house belongs to another Jew, with the
same name: Simon. But his host's trade is not respectable in the eyes of strict Jews. His host is a leatherworker, and that trade can easily bring a man into con-
tact with the skins of animals regarded by strict Jews as
unclean. Is this a proper house to stay in? And the view
from the roof is also disturbing. The harbour is full of
ships, some with their sails hoisted for voyages which are
about to take their unknown cargoes to unknown ports
around the Mediterranean. Are those sails hoisted for
trade which is clean? Is this a proper world to live in?

On this roof – to provide some cover from the noon-
day glare and heat – is an awning, itself rather like a sail.
In its shade Simon tries to pray, but with this confusion
in his mind he feels nothing like his nickname, 'Rock'. His
thoughts wander around his problems. He is also hungry,
and can smell dinner being prepared downstairs. He
dozes off.

In a dream, he sees uncleanness: all kinds of animals,
reptiles, and wild birds. Most of them are forbidden food
to Jews. This alarming collection is all in a large sheet –
a white sail, the awning above him. It is lowered so that
it almost touches Simon the Rock. It is lowered three

times. And God himself seems to be letting this thing down. And there is a voice: 'Get up, Rock; kill and eat!'

This dream shows the nervousness, even disgust, produced in the mind of a devout Jew by any kind of involvement in the non-Jewish world. But it also shows the power of the new vision of the world. For in the dream, Peter naturally replies: 'Certainly not, Lord! I have never eaten anything considered defiled or unclean.' But he hears the voice saying: 'Do not consider anything unclean that God has declared clean.' The God and Father of Jesus Christ, now controlling the deepest level of Simon the Rock's personality, is the God who makes and controls all: animals, reptiles, wild birds, trading ships, the people of the world. To serve such a God means being ready to go into the world. More, it means being ready to find evidence of God's work and victories throughout the world, and being ready to say: 'Who was I . . . to try to stop God!' (11:17) The world which seems so bewildering and threatening is God's – and is clean!

Racial prejudice is well known to be a major force in the modern world. Most blatantly it is the prejudice of the white man against the coloured man, with a physical revulsion against mixed marriages. But the coloured man is also bitter against the white man, and the relationships between Africans and Asians are often tense. The increasing need to live with people of other races produces nervousness and disgust – almost exactly as Simon Peter felt about non-Jews. And these feelings are often linked with a fear of the future in a world which seems bound to be increasingly mixed up. But sometimes friendship and even marriage leap across the racial gap. And then people know that to honour humanity is to be colour-blind.

As the twenty-first century draws nearer, we stand on the brink of a future which must be revolutionary. The richer nations hesitate before entering a world of new cities and new industries: it may be an affluent world, but it is very frightening. The poorer nations face prospects which are even more enigmatic and terrifying, thanks to overpopulation. All nations know that the future will not offer unlimited *natural* resources – and ask themselves whether *human* resources are adequate. When oil

runs out, will man's courage too? No wonder that so
many lack confidence in the future! But sometimes
modern people feel that they are moving into the future –
and are rising to its challenges. In their excited confidence
such people get close to Simon Peter's vision of a world
which will be far richer than his familiar world, but
where, after all, he will feel at home.

In chapter 16, a superior leather-worker specializing not
in tanning skins but in making tents is found in the port
of Troas (on the west coast of the modern Turkey). One
reason why his trade is needed is that the Roman army
uses many tents. Indeed this man, like his father, has the
honour, rare outside Italy, of being a Roman citizen. Saul
comes from Tarsus, a university and business town five
hundred miles away. Like his father he has been trained
as a member of the Jewish *élite*, the Pharisees, but he has
a mind which makes him a citizen of the whole cultural
world of the Roman empire. Accordingly he uses the
Roman name, Paulus.
Since becoming a Christian Paul has travelled far, in
more senses than one. But we gather he has never been
to Greece – although that country, too, now belongs to
the Roman empire, and although this port of Troas is
constantly in touch with the northern province of Greece,
Macedonia. Near by are the ruins of the ancient city of
Troy. In the first Christian century these ruins are hidden
under a large mound – they are not to be excavated until
1870 – but to be civilized means to know Homer's poetry
on the wars of the Greeks and Trojans. We can imagine
how, when walking on the quay, Paul has looked with
curiosity on the people from Macedonia, some of them
looking the very opposite of Homer's heroes. Now it is
night, and he is asleep in this thought-provoking Troas.
In his sleep, he dreams. He saw a man of Macedonia
standing and begging him, 'Come over to Macedonia
and help us!' That dream is enough. As a companion was
to write: 'As soon as Paul had this vision, we got ready to
leave for Macedonia, because we decided that God had
called us to preach the Good News to the people there.'
So a leader of the Christian Church sets foot for the first
time on European soil.

And something of that experience has come to anyone who has really become involved with 'foreigners'. As a child one looks at TV or at stamps or at maps, and one wonders what these countries are really like. How does it *feel* to live in such remote places? Later on one takes a holiday or a job abroad. There are the problems of travel, accommodation, language. But eventually in that 'foreign' country one feels more or less at home – and gradually one sees for oneself how little national frontiers matter on this planet.

This book, then, gives us someone about to eat unfamiliar food, someone about to go to an unfamiliar country. The only difference from our everyday experience is that these scenes, which we can easily understand and enjoy, are turning-points in mankind's spiritual life. Here decisions are made which will shape the future, as Christianity faces one crisis after another in its expedition into the world. And the author of *Acts* is perfectly well aware of the wider significance of his stories. He is a man with a philosophy of history. This is what makes his book far more than a history book.

The first Christian century was felt by many at the time to be full of dangers. The world was being forced into a new unity with bewildering swiftness, and the life of the mind was becoming cosmopolitan like politics and economics. The Roman empire was able to crush anti-colonial revolts (such as the revolt which was to bring the Jews in Palestine to disaster in the year 70). But the gigantic new state, so much bigger than anything the world had seen before, was under great stresses. The emperors in Rome, wielding unprecedented power, were often either wicked or weak; for their subjects, both conditions were equally dangerous. The army which maintained the state by blood and iron was liable to mutiny against the civil authorities. And despite many technical advances a bad harvest was a big blow to the supplies needed to feed the growing population – so much so that we read in *Acts* (11:28) that one of the Christians named Agabus 'predicted that a great famine was about to come over all the earth'. Although no universal famine occurred, there were many local famines.

But deeper than anything else there was a widespread hunger for truth – not for truth of the technical, political, commercial, or military kind (there were plenty of these truths available in the Roman empire), but for truth to feed the spirit of man. It was a time of religious chaos and spiritual vacuum.

In every one of these ways, the first century is uncannily like the twentieth. In the first century (as has been said) Christianity 'out-lived, out-thought, and out-died' its opponents. The crisis of the Roman empire ended in the fourth century with the Church's triumph – and the seeds of this triumph were sown in the age of *Acts*. But if the present world crisis is to end in anything like a similar victory for Christianity, some very hard challenges will have to be faced.

Some of the twentieth-century challenges to Christianity are geographical. *Is this religion which since the first century has been so intimately associated with the history of Europe (for better or for worse) really going to take root in countries which increasingly reject the white man?*

In chapter 8 of *Acts*, a Christian evangelist, Philip, finds 'an important official in charge of the treasury of the Queen, or Candace, of Ethiopia' – reading aloud as he rides in a carriage along the road south from Jerusalem to Gaza, the road home. That African from 'Ethiopia' (the area now called the Sudan) appears to have been converted to Judaism already. Rapidly he becomes a Christian. But *Acts* does not follow Christianity's progress in Africa. For all we know, very little progress was made in the first Christian century. Perhaps that unnamed African, who then 'continued on his way, full of joy', had not gathered enough from Philip about Christianity to be able to share his joy as an evangelist when he got home? At any rate, Philip promptly returned to Palestine. But thanks to innumerable evangelists Christianity is now present, and under challenge, in most parts of Africa – in Egypt and the Sudan, in the real Ethiopia, down to the Cape and across the Sahara to the coasts of the Atlantic.

The word 'Asia' is found in *Acts*. However, in the first century it meant only one province in the Roman empire – the western coast and part of the interior, of the modern Turkey, which is also called by the geographers 'Asia

Minor'. We know Asia as the continent where the majority of the human race lives – and where in almost every country the Christian Church has small branches, thanks to heroic efforts mainly in the nineteenth and twentieth centuries.

The question now is this: can Christianity flourish in Africa or Asia as it has done in Europe and the Americas – and perhaps in a purer form?

And other challenges to twentieth-century Christianity are social. *Is this religion which has so often been the religion of the privileged really going to take root in the age of democracy?*

In *Acts*, Christianity begins with a congregation of humble people in Jerusalem. Most of the men were (one imagines) labourers. Their poverty was so real that when anyone with possessions joined the congregation, it was the custom to sell those possessions 'and distribute the money among all, according to what each one needed' (2:45). This putting into practice of the motto 'to each one according to his need' (4:35) can be called communism if one likes, provided that one remembers that the motives were not political and that the disposal of private property was neither compulsory (5:4) nor complete (12:12). Quite soon in *Acts* (11:29) the poverty of the church in Jerusalem becomes so acute that richer Christian congregations decide to send Christian aid to it.

After such beginnings, it is ominous that the first European to be converted by Paul, a woman named Lydia, is 'a dealer in purple goods' (16:14). Purple garments were then a luxury for rich people – and purple was the imperial colour, the colour of power. Lydia's trade is ominous because when Christianity became the official religion of the Roman empire, it fell a victim to the Roman disease of regimentation. In the dark ages after the fall of that empire, the Church took over some of the functions of the state – and some of its style. Instead of a close fellowship, the emphasis was now on law and discipline under the bishops (who wore purple). Instead of a generous sharing which was a model and rebuke to a selfish society, the Church became identified with the economic system of the time with its rigid divisions between the privileged and the 'have-nots'. For example, some bishops owned serfs (or slaves). The change from the beginnings in Jerusalem could not be more striking. The Church conquered the Roman empire – and, spiritually, was its victim. And the question now is: can Christianity stop being purple?

And other challenges to twentieth-century Christianity are intellectual. *Is this religion which became the faith of so many thinkers and artists in the European (and American) past really going to take root afresh in the age of science and technology?*

In Chapter 17, Paul addresses a sceptical audience in Athens. 'He seems to be talking about foreign gods.' That was what the audience thought of him before he spoke – and after his speech, still 'some . . . made fun of him.' Gradually Christianity did convert the intellectuals (beginning with Dionysius in Athens that day); but it now seems to have lost most of them, so that to modern-minded people the news brought by Paul to Europe once again often seems foreign or comic. Perhaps part of the trouble comes precisely because Christianity was in the end so successful in converting those Greek philosophers. It scored a great success – and we have to pay the price. For the converted Greeks expressed the news about Jesus of Nazareth in the language of Greek philosophy derived from Plato and Aristotle, and the original Christian convictions were made highly abstract and complicated in order to be respectable philosophically. Even today many Christians are convinced that orthodox Christianity must be expressed in that Greek style, and we pay the price that Christianity seems to be outdated intellectually. In the age of science, the question is this. Can what is essential in Christianity be recovered in its original simplicity, and believed anew with all the heart and mind?

Finally, many psychological challenges arise inside the life of the Christian Church. *Can this Church which has become old be made new?*

We read in this book that 'the group of believers was one in mind and heart.' (4:32) We look around us, and see Christians divided into separate denominations and conflicting schools of thought. (The rivalry of the churches in Jerusalem itself has been specially notorious.)

We read of the 'great power' in that primitive community – but when we look around we find the churches too often impotent. We read of 'glad and humble hearts' (2:46) – and we know that Christians have too often varied between conceit and gloom. It is one of the marks of greatness in *Acts* that its author does not pretend that the early Christians were always in agreement, or that they were never puzzled. It is a human church that is described here. But it is a church which is intensely alive, and its liveliness causes a stir. As enemies complain: 'These men have caused trouble everywhere!' (17:6)

It is a melancholy business to study the map of St Paul's journeys, and to ask oneself what has happened to the Christian communities which he founded in Asia Minor. Many of them could not survive (at least, not in any strength) when the Muslim religion, Islam, swept through – just as the rich farms and cities of Roman times could not survive when the forests of the area were cut down, the rainfall was disastrously reduced, and the good soil was blown away. We ask: can Christianity stop being white, can it stop being purple, can it stop being Greek? But an even more urgent question now is: can spiritual vitality be recovered, can the green return to the Christian Church?

Acts provides no ready-made answers to these twentieth-century questions. But it contains some clues worth studying by those who are interested chiefly in modern questions – not in the details of life under the Romans.

The author of *Acts* is obviously glad and proud to tell the story of these heroic times. But there is a danger here. If we regard *Acts* as a record of the good old days, and then pile on top of that all the thousands of books which have been written about the history of Christianity since its beginnings, we are in danger of creating for ourselves the impression that the good old days were far, far better than anything that is possible now or in the future. So treated, the Christian past feeds nostalgia – and nostalgia eventually becomes a handicap in our own job, which is to live now. This is the tragedy when Christian history is misused.

If we look at *Acts* carefully we shall find it refreshing

because in this book Christianity is liberated from the
dead weight of the past.

In chapter 15, there is a brief report of a 'long debate'
in Jerusalem. The debate is about the terms on which
Gentile converts are to be admitted into the Church. A
new world is opening up with the arrival of all these
non-Jews, and not surprisingly the conservatives in
Jerusalem are alarmed. The conservative argument is:
'They have to be circumcised and told to obey the Law of
Moses.' In other words, the new Christians must accept
not only the Lord Jesus but also a package consisting of
the whole Jewish heritage, assembled over two thousand
years. In the end, Simon Peter and James the brother of
Jesus – the very men who might have been expected to
stand firm as pillars of conservatism – take the lead in
allowing freedom to the new Christians. James sums it
up: 'It is my opinion . . . that we should not trouble the
Gentiles who are turning to God.' The new Christians can
live their own lives.

It would be unfair (although tempting!) to interpret
that very radical and very brave decision in Jerusalem as
necessarily meaning that the whole *Christian* heritage is
not to be insisted on when twentieth-century people turn
to God. But at least this account of the first council in the
Church's history frees us to face our questions in a radical
and brave spirit.

It is suggestive that in the whole of the discussion as
recorded in chapter 15, no appeal is made to Jesus's own
words as settling the matter, although the Old Testament
is quoted by James. Perhaps Jesus's own teaching was
analysed with great care – but if so, that is not recorded.
As a matter of fact, Jesus's teaching may not have settled
problems about the possible admission of Gentiles to the
community of his followers. Jesus had worked among his
fellow-Jews, but the gospels include some traditions of a
gentle and welcoming attitude to Gentiles. (Particularly
is this the tone of Luke's gospel. For example, the sermon
by Jesus in his home-synagogue at Nazareth, about the
'Spirit of the Lord' and 'Good News to the poor',
includes pointed reminders that the great prophets of
Israel, Elijah and Elisha, were 'sent' to foreigners [4:16-
27.]) Probably the question of Gentiles becoming 'believers'

was left open by Jesus – so that different answers to the questions could be given by equally devoted believers. But in any case, *Acts* contains no suggestion that the question was settled by arguing about what Jesus had said.

Instead of thinking that the rules are already laid down, the Christians struggle to discover the right policy. Simon Peter recalls how God has acted in recent years, and James suggests a fresh solution to the problems involved. And when these decisions are put into a letter, the startling claim is made: 'The Holy Spirit and we have agreed . . .'

Without misusing this story to justify our own decision, we can see it as a promise that the power will come from God to those who in new circumstances pray and debate in order to find new wisdom. But we can also note that this promise is made to the Christian fellowship, met to pray with deep devotion and to talk in the spirit of charity, under the guidance of the experienced apostles. The promise is not made to the isolated individual, or to the irresponsible rebel.

This book tells of no more than the first steps in the right direction. It is called *The Acts of the Apostles*. That is a misleading title. The book says very little about the apostles apart from Peter, later to be joined by James the brother of Jesus and more excitingly by Paul the ambassador of Jesus to the non-Jewish world. A better title would be *The Acts of Peter and Paul*. And the book is in many other ways highly selective. No report is included about any Christian mission in Galilee, which was still full of people who had heard Jesus teach and who had been cured by him. *Acts* mentions the church in Galilee very casually (9:31). Nothing is said about how the congregation was built up in Alexandria, then the second city of the Roman empire, said to contain a million Jews. No support (or denial) is given to the fascinating traditions which were handed down the Church that the apostle Thomas became a missionary among the Parthians (towards Russia) and in India. There is no account of the beginnings of Christianity in Spain or in Gaul (the modern France). These silences disappoint our curiosity, when the book begins by bringing together a crowd of Jews seeming to cover the known world. 'We are from Parthia, Media, and Elam; from Mesopotamia, Judea, and Cappadocia; from Pontus and Asia, from Phrygia and Pamphylia, from Egypt and the regions of Libya near Cyrene; some of us are from Rome . . . from Crete and Arabia . . .' (2:9-11)

It seems that *Acts* is so selective because its aim is to show how Paul came to be on a ship from Jerusalem to Rome. The early Christians believed that only *some* missionary work was needed. God would decide when enough warning had been given, and then he could send Jesus to be the Judge of all. All mankind would see Jesus when normal history finished. 'Then the Son of Man will appear, coming in a cloud with great power and glory.' (*Luke* 21:27) According to this belief, the journey from Jerusalem to Rome, taking the Christian message to the very centre of the known world, was simply the most important part of the limited Christian mission. It was the grandest gesture of the Christians before the End: a gesture of faith and obedience, made in the most public circumstances possible. It was also the most dramatic invitation possible, urging all to repent before the End. But it was left to Jesus himself, the Judge of all, the Son of Man in power and glory, to deal with mankind at the End.

That explains why *Acts* is not interested in telling us about every expansion of the Church. Nor does *Acts* suggest that the Church *ought* to expand everywhere at once. On the contrary, it says that 'the Holy Spirit did not let them preach . . . in the province of Asia' – or in the next province (16:6, 7). And *Acts* is not really interested in counting the heads of converts. To be sure, some figures are given early on: 'about one hundred and twenty' (1:15), 'about three thousand' (2:41), 'about five thousand' (4:4). Christianity starts with quite a big bang – whether or not these figures are accurate. But soon it is enough to say 'more and more' (5:14), and when Paul eventually does work in 'Asia' the vague claim is made that 'all the people who lived in the province of Asia, both Jews and Gentiles, heard the word of the Lord.' (19:10) The author of *Acts* seems to have shared the belief of the early Christians that numbers do not matter. Being 'witnesses' does – before the End.

The End did not come as quickly as the first Christians expected. They were ardent in this expectation and prayer – as we are reminded by almost the last words in *The Revelation to John*. ' "I am coming soon!" So be it. Come, Lord Jesus!' (22:20) But their prayer was not granted. History continued, with all its confusion, anxiety, suffering, and tragedy. A bitter disappointment must lie behind those words which are put simply and calmly at the beginning of *Acts* (1:6, 7). Question: 'Lord, will you at this time give the Kingdom back to Israel?' Answer: 'The times and occasions are set by my Father's own authority, and it is not for you to know when they will be.' But *Acts* goes far beyond this disappointment. Its purpose is to show the meaning within history of what are in fact the last words of *The Revelation to John*: 'May the grace of the Lord Jesus be with all.'

The story in *Acts* of the journey from Jerusalem to Rome is indeed the clue to what is most important in all the world's history. For it shows how 'the grace of the Lord Jesus' can be known on every road, to the ends of the earth and to the end of time. *Acts* helped the second-generation Christians to break away from the belief that the End was bound to come soon. The apostles are given orders for a long trek, 'in Jerusalem, in all of Judea and Samaria, and to the ends of the earth' (1:6-8). *Acts* showed – or vividly reminded – Christians that history was much more than a short pause before the End. To the man or woman who follows Jesus through it, history is full of meaning.

In the days when he lived as a man in Palestine, Jesus made himself known to Peter and the other disciples. But that was not the end. It is significant that John's gospel (the last to be written, after much Christian experience) ends with Jesus still saying to Peter: 'Follow me!' (21:22) The implication is that, wherever Peter goes, he will find that Jesus has been there before. And *Acts* is a book which shows this happening.

Luke's gospel includes the famous picture of the Emmaus road, when after his death 'Jesus himself drew near and walked along with them.' (24:15) *Acts* tells (three times!) of the shattering experience on the Damascus road when Jesus draws near to Saul of Tarsus. He stays near. One night in Corinth – a seaport so famous for its vices that there was a suggestive phrase in Greek, 'to corinthize' – Paul dreams of Jesus, and hears the message. 'Do not be afraid, but keep on speaking and do not give up, because I am with you. No one will be able to harm you, because many in this city are my people.' (18:9, 10) Dreaming in a prison in Jerusalem, Paul hears the same voice: 'Courage! You have given your witness to me here in Jerusalem, and you must do the same in Rome also.' (23:11) And the courage which Paul derives from this conviction is better than a soldier's armour when the road to Rome takes him over the sea and into a violent storm; and through that storm to trial and, in the end, death.

Since the days of Peter and Paul, the same conviction that one follows an active, mobile Lord has produced the same courage in people who walk the lanes, roads, streets, avenues of all the continents. *Acts* leaves us with the correct impression that a faith able to survive and to conquer by *this* road is able to make any journey in the world – until the End which to the first Christians seemed so near does come, and the acts of the followers of Jesus are completed.

For this reason, the following of Jesus was in the early years referred to simply as 'the Way'. The phrase occurs six times in *Acts*. It might be good to use the phrase more in our time, because it gives a sense of the vitality and the endless adventure. It preserves something of the dynamic confidence and the sheer thrill of the first Christians' message as it is summed up in (for example) Peter's command to the lame man: 'in the name of Jesus Christ of Nazareth I order you to walk!' (3:6) But even this phrase 'the Way' has its dangers. It may suggest that Christianity is a way of life – and no more. (The Chinese religious way of life, the *Tao*, is 'the Way'.) Or that this way is to be followed by using one's own intelligence and strength – and no more. Or that this way has been opened up by a dead teacher – and no more. Or that it is a code of discipline in religion – and no more. (The Jewish religious law is called by Jews *Halakha*, which means 'the

Way'.) And in fact Christianity often has been understood as a 'way' in one or other of those dangerous meanings. Such a religion or philosophy does not take the road mapped in *Acts*.

It was no accident that the followers of 'the Way' were called *Christians* or 'Christ-people', for they were always talking about Christ and so they received this nickname – mentioned by the Roman historian Tacitus, writing soon after the year 60. And it was no accident that 'it was at Antioch that the disciples were first called Christians' (11:26).

Antioch, the capital of the great province of Syria, was the third city in the Roman empire. It was a glittering mixture of commerce and culture, with spectacular temples and parks and with people of many nationalities jostling each other in its streets. To people with the pure morals of the Jews, it must have seemed a sink of iniquity. This was, we are told, the first place where a considerable number of Gentiles believed 'the Good News about the Lord Jesus' (11:20). So 'the Way' could no longer be regarded as an eccentric form of Judaism: it was seen as itself. But those who decided to follow 'the Way' with all the sophisticated confusion of Antioch around them knew – better than people in more ordered circumstances – that they had to do more than follow a way of life. First, last, and all the time, they had to be people following Jesus their Lord. In a place such as Antioch, Christianity could not survive except as a personal relationship between the Christian and Christ.

The great clue to our problems provided by *Acts* is that there is now always a way, leading into the future – and it is the Way where Jesus himself leads, filling his followers with power as he promised (1:8). Such a way can be trusted to take Christians into the whole modern world, into the age of democracy and science, with the secret of inexhaustible energy.

This clue is not expanded in *Acts* into an elaborate theology. No, the secret is left for each person to discover, for the words of the hymn echo the message of *Acts*:

For none can guess its grace,
Till he become the place
Wherein the Holy Spirit makes his dwelling.

Instead of providing a theological system, what *Acts* does
is to make clear that the Holy Spirit is far greater than the
neat prisons in which Christians have wanted to pin their
religion down. We ought to notice how *Acts* shows the
Spirit cutting across many of the divisions all too
familiar in the history of Christianity.

The people who defend the *status quo* or the Establish-
ment are in *Acts* the enemies of Christianity – not its
representatives! It is an exciting book, full of action – and
full of the deeper kind of excitement which creates the
courage leading to deliberate, persistent action. As one
indication of this, in the teaching given in this book there
is no emphasis on the dull duty to 'be good'. On the other
hand, the people who join the Christian Way do become
'good' – so much so that the world begins to take notice.
And they take a delight in their regular meetings with
each other in order to worship the God who has poured
out this new life on them through Jesus Christ. In this
book there is no place for slackness – and it is not
surprising that these Christians are compared in Paul's
letters with soldiers and athletes.

In *Acts*, the whole emphasis is on practical life. Mere
theory or speculation is excluded. In the modern phrase,
this book is existentialist, for it is a book about the
existence of people: their problems, their decisions, their
acts. It is also an open-minded and generous book. It
acknowledges human and natural goodness everywhere.
Peter says: 'I now realize that it is true that God treats all
men on the same basis. Whoever fears him and does
what is right is acceptable to him.' (10:34-5) But there is
nothing vague or flabby here. *Acts* is a book of doctrine –
and proud of it. The core of this book is this: 'We are
here to announce the Good News.' (14:15) It is news
about 'the power of the name of Jesus Christ of Nazareth',
and 'salvation is to be found through him alone.'
(4:10, 12) For in comparison with this power which
liberates, all the righteousness in the world seems dirty
and all the happiness in the world seems shallow. *Acts*

prepares us to understand what Paul writes to Philippians about the Lord Jesus: 'For his sake I have thrown everything away; I consider it all as mere garbage.' (3:8)

This is a book where individuals and groups are decidedly different from each other. There are many personalities in these pages, and they sometimes clash. There are also many local groups not placed under an elaborate code of discipline. There is nothing uniform or even tidy about the Christian life which throbs in this book. The word 'church' (in Greek, *ekklesia*) is never used except as meaning the local Christian congregation, or once (9:31) 'the church throughout all of Judea, Galilee, and Samaria'. The Christian (or semi-Christian) congregation in no less a place than Alexandria, the capital of Egypt, appears to be so independent in its doctrine that more than twenty years after the crucifixion of Jesus one of its most intelligent members, Apollos, appears to know only the 'facts about Jesus' up to the crucifixion (18:25). Later we are told that many Christians in Jerusalem have heard only false rumours about Paul's missionary work (21:20-1).

However, *Acts* is also a book about unity. It was not a tightly organized unity, for it cannot have been easy for these individuals and groups to keep in touch. Travel was much more difficult then than it would be in our time. We are reminded of this at the end of *Acts*. Wanting to cross the eastern Mediterranean from Troas to Jerusalem – a distance of some seven hundred miles as the crow or the aeroplane flies – Paul has to take one ship which goes down the coast, then another which takes him via Cyprus to Tyre in Syria and waits a week to unload cargo; only after this delay does the voyage continue to Judea (21:1-7). More vividly, we are told in chapters 27 and 28 of the very slow and very dangerous voyage from Caesarea (in Palestine), via Myra (in Turkey), Crete, Malta, and Sicily to Puteoli (in Italy) – at the end of which the Jews in Rome inform Paul that they have had no letters or other news about him from Jerusalem. But the Roman empire had done something without precedent by building good roads (mainly for military purposes) and by imposing law and order on the Mediterranean countries. Although the little ships of the time had to hug the coasts, communications by road were relatively quick. The Christians took advantage of this.

Acts astonishes us by the extent to which the different congregations do keep in touch – and by the extent to which their unity is marked by mutual loyalty and love. For example, when reports about the reception of 'the Good News' in Antioch reached the church in Jerusalem (three hundred miles away), 'they sent Barnabas to Antioch.' (11:22) Later, when the Christians in Jerusalem experienced great poverty, the more affluent congregations in many places sent money to Jerusalem. For this book is about unity, as well as about freedom. The freedom here is freedom given by the man named Jesus, and the unity here comes because all belong to him as limbs belong to a body. In *Acts* what is technically called 'the Pauline doctrine of the Church as the Body of Christ' is not stated theologically, as Paul states it in his letters. But it is present in a nutshell. It is present in the belief that for Saul of Tarsus (or anyone else) to persecute any Christians is for him to persecute Jesus: 'Saul, Saul! Why do you persecute me?' (9:4) After that, whenever Paul saw a Christian he saw Jesus Christ.

And this is a book where the revolutionary novelty of the Christian message is stressed again and again. Here the Church ceases to be a part of the religion of the Jews – and so ceases to enjoy the tolerance extended by the Roman empire to Judaism as a *religio licita* (licensed religion). The break between Christianity and Judaism could scarcely be more dramatic. In Pisidian Antioch, Paul and Barnabas boldly shout to the Jews: 'we will leave you and go to the Gentiles.' (13:46) In Corinth, Paul shakes the dust from his clothes and exclaims to the Jews: 'If you are lost, you yourselves must take the blame for it! I am not responsible. From now on I will go to the Gentiles.' (18:6) To the Jews in Rome, Paul says: 'God's message of salvation has been sent to the Gentiles. They will listen!' (28:28)

But this is *not* a brutal radicalism, *not* a complete break. Chapter 16 shows Paul circumcising a young man, Timothy, whose father was a Gentile (and uncircumcised) but whose mother was a Jewess. That young man was wanted as a Christian missionary, and for the sake of peace it had to be made possible for Jews to treat him as fully one of them. Chapter 21 shows Paul performing a ceremony of purification in the temple at Jerusalem – and paying for four fellow-Jews to do the same. Chapter 23 shows Paul addressing the priests' council in Jerusalem. 'My brothers! I am a Pharisee, the son of Pharisees . . .' Chapter 24 shows Paul defending his Jewish orthodoxy. 'I . . . believe in all the things written in the Law of Moses and the books of the prophets.'

In the very middle of *Acts* (15:22-3), there is an appeal for toleration across the gap which separates Jews from Gentiles. We read a letter from 'the apostles and the elders, your brothers', in Jerusalem, 'to all brothers of Gentile birth who live in Antioch, Syria, and Cilicia'.

Very pointedly this letter does *not* insist on circumcision, which always has been for men the greatest visible sign that one is or has become a Jew. But it contains these 'necessary rules': 'eat no food that has been offered to idols; eat no blood; eat no animal that has been strangled; and keep yourselves from immorality.' We do not know precisely what is meant here by 'immorality'; many scholars think that it refers only to marriage within the degrees of relationship prohibited by the Jewish law. The other rules seem designed to make it easier for Christians of Jewish and of Gentile origins to eat together. We all know that another race's habits at table are particularly likely to arouse prejudices. So this letter tells the Gentile Christians to avoid hurting Jewish feelings by accepting the most important of the Jewish customs about food. The letter is nowhere mentioned in Paul's letters, and despite what *Acts* claims (16:4) it may have been a local, temporary affair. But it stands as a wise piece of advice about good manners as a part of Christian love.

There has been much argument among modern scholars as to whether *Acts* exaggerates the break between the churches and the synagogues. Or does it exaggerate Paul's own loyalty to Judaism? Obviously the details of this tangled situation do give scope for scholarly debates about what Paul and the others really did feel. Paul himself tells the Corinthians in his first letter that while he is free to act as he thinks right he is determined not to give offence. So 'while working with the Jews, I live like a Jew', but 'when with Gentiles I live like a Gentile.' (9:20, 21) Before such freedom could be reached, there were many uncertainties and controversies. It has often been suggested that the author of *Acts* underestimates these, which may well be the case – he does not sound like a man who has been caused agony by the problem. But *Acts* does not mislead us when it says that the Christian fellowship works the problem out. Here is a fellowship which, despite some quarrels, does know how to combine an insistence on the newness of its news with a sensitivity to the traditional and the slow-moving.

In this book, the Christians throw away their inhibitions. 'These men are drunk!' is a natural comment for people to make when they observe the extraordinary behaviour of the apostles after the first exciting inrush of the Holy Spirit (2:13). Later, 'the members of the Council were amazed to see how bold Peter and John were' (4:13). But it is stranger still that Christianity – which began as a religious group or sect consisting of a few fishermen and others more or less as poor, and which recruited few who were wise, or powerful, or of high social standing (as Paul reminded the Corinthians in his first letter to them [1:26]) – so quickly became involved in educated arguments.

One explanation is that even fishermen from Galilee were not literally 'ordinary men of no education', whatever the learned priests said (4:13). They had been educated to know and to discuss the Old Testament – and that is precisely what Peter and the others did in order to present their message to their fellow-Jews. Another explanation is that Saul of Tarsus was undeniably an educated citizen of the Roman empire. He was perfectly willing to proclaim his message in language which Greeks would understand, debating with 'certain Epicurean and Stoic teachers' of philosophy and quoting the poet Aratus (17:18, 28). In Ephesus he found it natural to make his headquarters in the university: 'every day he held discussions in the lecture hall of Tyrannus.' (19:9) He was also very ready to argue in his own defence in the law courts up to the supreme tribunal: 'I appeal to the Emperor.' (25:11) Even Festus acknowledged that Paul was under the influence of books, not of alcohol, when he shouted at him: 'You are mad, Paul! Your great learning is driving you mad!' (26:24) But the sermons delivered by Peter and the disputations conducted by Paul are only typical of a general confidence in the power of Christianity to stand up to critical examination. In *Acts*, the Holy Spirit destroys shyness – but is not the enemy of reasoning.

So often Christianity has been presented in a way which tries to make us choose. *Either* respectability *or* chaos! *Either* being practical *or* being dogmatic! *Either* variety *or* unity! *Either* radicalism *or* conservatism! *Either* being enthusiastic *or* being reasonable! But *Acts* refuses to make any of these choices. It shows what the tensions were in the life of the first Christian generation – but it also shows how they were overcome. It is a book about a big God, a big Christ, a big Church.

2. ANGELS AND HANDKERCHIEFS

But what kind of a book is *Acts*? Is it pious propaganda, or is it history? The question must occur to modern readers of a passage such as this: 'God was performing unusual miracles through Paul. Even handkerchiefs and aprons he had used were taken to the sick, and their diseases were driven away and the evil spirits would go out of them.' (19:11, 12) The 'aprons' would have been used by Paul in his work as a tent-maker, and the 'handkerchiefs' were probably his sweat-rags. But these human touches are found alongside a reference to diseases being caused by devils. We ask whether we are in the real world, or in the world imagined by superstition.

The same question is likely to strike us when we read the account of Peter's liberation from prison in chapter 12. It begins with Peter sleeping between two guards, chained to them. It ends with Peter knocking on the door and Rhoda answering. But in between these down-to-earth details come a rescuing angel and a miraculously opening iron gate. We can sympathize with Peter who, we read, 'did not know ... if what the angel was doing was real'.

To answer this question about *Acts*, we must understand that it is a book written by someone with a passionate belief that God controls history – and it is a book about people who share this belief. In chapter 17, we find the Jewish and Christian belief in God proclaimed to men of Athens, who at this stage are sympathetic: 'God, who made the world and everything in it ... does not need anything that men can supply by working for him, since it is he himself who gives life and breath and everything else to all men.' In chapter 4, we find a window opened into the heart of the Christian Church as described in *Acts*, for we read the prayer: 'Master and Creator of heaven, earth, and sea, and all that is in them! ... Stretch out your hand to heal, and grant that wonders and miracles may be performed ...'

The speeches in *Acts*, long and short, from Peter's in

Jerusalem to Paul's in Rome, all proclaim the same conviction that God is the Master of events. The crucifixion
of Jesus would not have taken place, had God not
allowed it. 'God, in his own will and knowledge, had
already decided that Jesus would be handed over to
you.' (2:23) God could never be defeated, so 'God
raised him from the dead.' (2:24) And the same rule
extends all over the earth, for God 'fixed beforehand the
exact times and the limits of the places where they would
live' and now 'he has fixed a day in which he will judge
the whole world with justice . . .' (17:26, 31)

God's rule extends down to details – as *Acts* reminds us
again and again with its stories of the providential
ordering of events. The end of his letter to the Romans
shows that before his last visit to Jerusalem Paul was
worried about whether or not his work would prove
acceptable to the Christian leaders there, but was looking
forward to a visit to Rome – 'full of joy, if it is God's will'
– on his way to missionary work in Spain (15:22-33). In
the event, according to *Acts*, Paul was accepted by the
church in Jerusalem (somewhat nervously) – but also
beaten up by the Jews and assisted by the Romans, so
that he saw Rome as a prisoner who had felt compelled
to exercise his right as a Roman citizen to appeal to the
Emperor. The implication in *Acts* is clear: Paul did not
expect what happened, yet it turned out to be God's will.
The end of *Acts* is, indeed, a great hymn of praise to God
who orders all things.

This fervent belief in the sovereignty of God was
expressed in a time when the reality of evil spirits, angels,
and miracles was almost everywhere taken for granted.

Pagans and Jews alike are shown by *Acts* (as by much
other evidence) to have shared this outlook with the early
Christians and with Jesus himself. In Samaria we meet a
conjuror, Simon, who so impressed 'all classes of society'
that he was known as 'The Great Power' (8:9-13). In
Cyprus we meet another magician, called ironically
enough 'Bar-Jesus' (Son of Joshua) – 'a friend of the
Governor of the island, Sergius Paulus, who was an
intelligent man' (13:6, 7). In Philippi we meet 'a slave
girl who had an evil spirit in her that made her predict the
future' (16:16). In Ephesus we meet 'seven sons of a

Jewish High Priest named Sceva' who were driving out
evil spirits (19:14). Almost everyone then accepted what
we call the 'supernatural'. The result was that when
people believed in a wonderfully powerful and good God,
they expected to see events involving evil spirits and
guardian angels and wonderful exceptions to the
ordinary course of events. When people marvelled at
God's active love, they expected to see miracles. When
people began reading a history of *The Acts of the Apostles*,
they did not stop reading when 'two men dressed in
white' suddenly appeared (1:10). They recognized them
as angels.

This is still the outlook of many people in the twentieth
century. Many millions of people in Asia, Africa and
elsewhere, including the West, accept the 'supernatural'
and think of themselves as being surrounded by good and
bad spirits, 'luck', 'fate', and so forth. Reports of miracles
are believed easily. Many Christians (even in the West)
have much the same convictions, even when most of their
neighbours think it superstitious to believe in the 'supernatural'. Such Christians feel perfectly at home in the
world described in *Acts*, and they find it difficult to
believe that any other attitude is truly religious.

Other Christians, however, find it very difficult or
impossible to believe in angels, devils or miracles,
because they accept the scientific view which is normal
among educated people today. For them, something
more needs to be said if they are to appreciate *Acts*. But
it is surely possible to believe in a wonderful God without
believing in 'wonders' which contradict science and
which in principle could never be fitted into science. Let
us take this question of Paul's handkerchiefs.

Paul must have been a man whose whole personality
radiated faith in God and love for his fellow-Christians,
and he must have been a man of great courage. It is
reasonable to suppose that the influence of such a man
made many people stronger, psychologically and even
physically. And even his handkerchiefs could be vivid
reminders of his personality. However, to give this
rational explanation is *not* to say that there is 'nothing in'
the claim that faith can heal. There is a vital truth in that
claim – the truth that one's mental attitude has profound

consequences for one's physical condition. And there is abundant evidence that faith has healed many diseases and still does in our own time (just as a lack of mental health causes many physical illnesses). So we can begin to understand how *faith* can make a lame man walk: 'it was faith in Jesus that made him well.' (3:16) At a time when Lydda is chiefly known as Israel's international airport, it is not incredible that in Lydda an invalid really was told by Peter to 'get up and make your bed' (9:34) – and did so.

Nor ought we to limit the possibility of healing to the exact limits of medical knowledge. No sensible doctor claims that everything is known, that every return to health must always be precisely as described in the current medical text-books. Healing which doctors cannot understand is perfectly possible. The only point we are making is that religion need not contradict science. Faith-healing, or 'divine' healing which no one can understand, can be believed in if the evidence is strong – without attacking the medical profession.

Or let us take the question of Peter's angel. Peter, like Paul, must have had some dramatic escapes from the enemies of Christianity. He probably had what we should call 'astonishing luck'. It is the easiest thing in the world for stories to grow about the escapes of such a hero. In fact Peter may have escaped while his guards slept – and the gate may have been left unlocked. However, to say this is *not* to say there is 'nothing in' stories of astonishing luck. Many people have told such stories because of what really did happen to them, and many such stories are told in our own time (for example, about war-time adventures). The only point we are making is that not every detail in all stories of 'astonishing luck' need be taken literally.

People in *Acts* talked about 'miracles' when they really were experiencing intensely the power and goodness of God. For such people, the natural healing processes and the natural means of survival and escape would be made suddenly quicker and easier – but in ways which scientifically minded people can in principle understand. Thus the lame man who walks at Peter's command in chapter 3 may have walked because of a new confidence produced by the faith which Peter spreads. The young man who falls from a window and is revived by Paul's hug in chapter 20 may not have been killed by the fall. His recovery may be an example of first-century First Aid!

People in *Acts* talked of 'angels', or may have had dreams or visions of 'angels', when they really were experiencing God's marvellous love. *Angelos* in Greek meant 'messenger', and we know that people in that age thought it more respectful to refer to God's messenger than to refer to God himself. Thus in chapter 7 Stephen says that 'angels' appeared to Moses in the burning bush and handed down God's law, when the Old Testament does not hesitate to say that God confronted Moses and gave him the Ten Commandments and the rest of the 'law of Moses'. Of course it is impossible to prove that angels *cannot* exist or *cannot* speak or act (for we cannot claim to understand the whole universe), but people who do not believe in angels are likely to conclude that to say 'an angel speaks' is a first-century way of saying 'God is present.'

A word needs to be added about the small number of occasions in *Acts* when people are said to be killed or harmed by miracles. These stories have special difficulty for people who believe that the divine Father is consistently the Source of love and healing. But the explanation may be that because of shock Ananias and Sapphira had fatal heart-attacks (5:1-11), and the magician denounced by Paul lost his sight for a time – as had happened to Saul of Tarsus himself (13:6-12).

Whatever may be our attitude to 'supernatural' marvels, surely what is important is the belief that God is 'Master and Creator of heaven, earth, and sea' – and is at work today. People of the kind that use handkerchiefs and aprons are changed by this belief. The vital claim in *Acts* is that 'they were all filled with the Holy Spirit and began to speak God's message with boldness' (4:31).

The whole of *Acts* is filled with the extraordinary power of the Holy Spirit, as 'the whole house' is said to have been filled by the Spirit 'when the day of Pentecost arrived in chapter 2. At least to the eye of faith, it is clear that God is doing something marvellous. It is put by Peter in a quotation from Joel in the Old Testament:

> your young men will see visions,
> and your old men will dream dreams.

What matters more, however, is that the middle aged will perform acts!

But here, too, a problem arises for those who are suspicious about miracles. According to *Acts*, when the Holy Spirit is given on the first Whitsunday, people from many different parts of the world, gathered in Jerusalem, hear the apostles speaking in their own languages. In fact all those people would have understood Hebrew, Greek or Latin. It is also a fact that nowhere else in *Acts* is use made of languages except Hebrew, Greek and Latin in order to communicate. On the contrary, it seems that Paul and Barnabas did not understand the local Lycaonian language used in Lystra, and only realized what was afoot – namely, sacrifice to them as gods – when people began doing things. Then Paul and Barnabas shouted, presumably in Greek (14:11-14). It is possible that on the first Whitsunday, the apostles made a great impression by using phrases picked up from many languages. But it seems more likely that the apostles babbled in uncontrolled excitement – so that people thought they were drunk. Their languages or 'tongues' were 'strange' in that sense. This seems to be what Paul is referring to in his first letter to the Corinthians (chapters 12-14), where 'the man who speaks in strange tongues helps only himself . . . unless there is someone present who can explain what he says.'

Why, then, does chapter 2 of *Acts* say that these 'strange tongues' were foreign languages? Presumably, it is in order to emphasize the international character of the fellowship of the Holy Spirit.

The Old Testament has the picture of the peoples of the world having to speak different languages as a punishment for their pride in building the great tower of Babel (*Genesis* 11:1-9). By painting this new picture where the peoples of the world are no longer divided by language, the author of *Acts* celebrates the international unity which comes after the humble acceptance of God's new message. And this is a picture which has great significance in the twentieth century. In our age, thanks to the new means of travel and communication and thanks to the new ecumenical fellowship (for example, the fellowship in the World Council of Churches), Christians living in different nations increasingly feel that they belong to one family. So the World Church is a foretaste of the One World.

There is no good reason to doubt that something strange did happen when the Christian Church was born. And one positive reason for believing that something happened is this: it has happened again and again when the Christian Church has been revived. Often there has been a revival of the excitement and ecstasy of the first Whitsunday, and often it has been accompanied by the joyful babbling for which the technical term, based on the Greek, is *glossolalia*. And this goes on in our own time. The 'Pentecostal' Churches and many 'independent' Churches in Africa and elsewhere now include millions of Christians, and they lay great emphasis on this. There is a wider Pentecostal movement in the main Churches, often called the 'charismatic' movement because *charisma* is the Greek for 'gift'; speaking in strange tongues is valued as one of God's best gifts.

What usually happens is that some Christians gather in an atmosphere of fellowship, enthusiasm and expectancy. There is hymn-singing, often with hand-clapping. There is a sermon, often supplemented by personal testimonies by converted members of the gathering. There is fervent prayer, not read from any book but often accompanied by the 'laying on of hands' with special prayers that the sick may be healed. Towards the end of the meeting, often after words of encouragement and promise, some of the Christians present 'speak in tongues' – although the experience may come without these preliminaries. The first experience of 'speaking in tongues' is often called being 'baptized with the Holy Spirit' – which is a quotation from *Acts* (1:5).

Even people who have not themselves been 'baptized with the Holy Spirit' can understand something – not everything – about the happiness it brings if they compare it with an audience's enthusiasm at a pop concert or with a crowd shouting at a football match. For this Pentecostal experience releases emotions which can otherwise be bottled up, and it binds all who share it together. It makes religion a living reality and a living community.

Having done our best to answer the question about the first Whitsunday, we may turn to the problem which arises for many in the very first chapter of *Acts*. We read that Jesus 'was taken up to heaven . . . and a cloud hid him from their sight' – which certainly seems to say that 'heaven' is above the clouds. And then 'two men dressed in white' assured the apostles that 'this Jesus, who was taken up from you into heaven, will come back in the same way . . .' – which seems to use the authority of angels in order to say that at his Second Coming Jesus will drop through the clouds like a spaceship. This is the picture of the Ascension of Jesus.

Two things may be stated with confidence about the apostles' experience after the death of Jesus. The first is that something strange happened to convince them that Jesus was the living Lord; it turned them from the people we meet in the gospels – people who understood little of what Jesus meant, and who deserted him – into the people we meet in *Acts*, people who first led the Christian Church in its courageous advance. The second is that from the surviving evidence we cannot gain a complete understanding of what happened. We are reminded how incomplete the evidence is when we note the differences of the accounts in the four gospels of the 'resurrection' appearances of Jesus – and specially when we observe how the four gospels all end differently. There seems to be a difference between the four gospels and *Acts*, which declares that 'for forty days after his death he showed himself to them many times' (1:3). This period of forty days is not mentioned in any of the gospels. Luke's gospel, for example, leaves the impression that Jesus was 'taken up into heaven' on the evening of the first Easter day (24:51), while John's gospel says that there were two more appearances after that day, although on that day the Holy Spirit was given (20:22). It is clear that although the first Christian generation was convinced of the reality of the resurrection of Jesus, many different traditions about its details were in circulation.

The ending of the 'resurrection' appearances in *Acts* is based somehow on the apostles' experience. It may be that this experience included seeing their risen Lord rising into the sky. Or it may be that *Acts* adds this bit in order to interpret the meaning of what was experienced – the 'resurrection' appearances which so strongly took place on the earth. If the figure of Jesus really was seen in the sky, that itself must have been an act of interpretation, for Jesus cannot literally have gone to live above the clouds. If this really took place, it was the last parable told by Jesus to teach his followers.

It teaches a number of extremely important lessons. First, the astounding 'resurrection' appearances are now over, and the followers of Jesus are not to spend their time waiting for more to happen. (One danger about attempts to communicate with the dead is that they may distract us from getting on with the business of living.) Second, Jesus is now invisible, which means that he is not confined to Palestine or to any other place: he belongs to the world. Third, Jesus has gone his way to the Father. He now shares the divine glory and power, which means that he can send the divine Spirit to his followers.

All this is put splendidly in other words at the end of Matthew's gospel: 'I have been given all authority in heaven and on earth. Go, then, to all peoples everywhere and make them my disciples . . . And remember! I will be with you always, to the end of the age.' But we need not believe that these actual words were spoken by the risen Jesus in the same way as he had taught before his death. That is, in fact, unlikely – for if those words about 'all peoples' (Matthew) and 'to the ends of the earth' (*Acts*) really had been the solemn last words of Jesus on earth, Christians such as Simon Peter would not have been so surprised to find God turning Gentiles into fellow-Christians. Surely the spiritual lesson taught by Matthew and *Acts* can be appreciated without taking all the details literally.

But, we may ask, what about this business of Jesus becoming a space-traveller? It is a way of saying that

Jesus goes to the heavenly Father. From the earliest known days in the history of religion, people have thought of the divine as being 'above' the human, the life of God as being 'above' the earth; and in many languages 'heaven', or the equivalent word for it, can mean either eternity or the sky. Of course, this is only one way of picturing God, for the divine is also 'in' the human and 'in' all things. But it is a way of thinking which arises naturally and inevitably from man's humility under the power and glory of God. If we picture God as being mainly 'in' us, we are liable to end up worshipping ourselves – or worshipping our society. If we picture God as being mainly 'in' the earth, we are liable to end up by worshipping the brute force in nature – or its blind fertility. Worship which is filled with a moral sensitivity is best pictured as the worship of God 'above' us. Just as the community which is created by God as Holy Spirit is above the divisions and quarrels of the world, so the very conviction that God is holy makes us want to lift our image of God high.

What, then, are we to make of the dramatic story of Saul's conversion? The story is so important in *Acts* that it is told three times (9:1-19, 22:6-16, 26:12-18). But it can puzzle modern readers, for it tells of a sudden light, a voice, and temporary blindness. We may also ask what relation it has to the 'resurrection' appearances which have been dramatically ended.

An examination shows that the evidence supplied by *Acts* is not completely clear. The point of the evidence is that Saul of Tarsus was converted in order to be an envoy for Christ to the Gentiles. But it is not made clear exactly how this mission was entrusted to him. In the first account, Ananias of Damascus is told in a vision that Saul will make the Lord's name known to the Gentiles. In the second, Ananias passes this message on to Saul. In the third, Saul is told by Jesus himself.

The first version of the story says that 'the men who were travelling with Saul . . . heard the voice,' but the second version contradicts this: 'The men with me saw the light but did not hear the voice.' We may guess that the voice was within Saul's mind – and we know that many people have heard voices in their minds. But what of the light? In the first and second versions it 'flashed', but in the third version 'I saw a light much brighter than the sun shining from the sky round me and the men travelling with me.' We may guess that it was not lightning, but an experience of Saul's somewhat similar to the 'flash of inspiration' of which many scientists and other thinkers, or artists, speak. We may guess that it was his convulsion that made the others kneel in fear. At the least, we may say that the evidence allows us to conclude that what happened to Saul on the Damascus road was a psychological experience. The story that he 'could not see a thing' until he had been baptized does not argue against this, for there have been many cases of temporary blindness for psychological causes.

This experience seems to have been a crisis of the whole personality. Tension may well have been building up for months or years. Paul's letters show that as a young man he ardently struggled to attain righteousness by keeping the whole of the Jewish religious law. *Acts* hints at this when it represents Paul as saying to a Jewish audience: 'I am a Jew, born in Tarsus of Cilicia, but brought up here in Jerusalem as a student of Gamaliel. I received strict instruction in the Law of our ancestors, and was just as dedicated to God as all of you here today are.' (22:3) But Saul of Tarsus did not find the peace of God along that way. On the contrary, the tension mounted.

What he heard about Jesus of Nazareth (whether or not he met Jesus) seems to have troubled him deeply, for Jesus possessed this peace – and overruled the Jewish law. What Saul saw of the lynching of Stephen seems to have brought his inner crisis to a head, although its first result was that 'Saul tried to destroy the church' in a frenzy of hatred. For the men who stoned Stephen to death had left their cloaks in Saul's charge (7:58), and 'Saul approved of his murder' (8:1). He could not get that out of his mind. Suddenly, on this road, the tension snapped. He knew in the depths of his being that his loyalty was to a Lord, not to a law – and that the name of this Lord was Jesus. It was as if Jesus had been goading him on, like a driver goading an ox. And it was as if he had been dashing himself against the driver's stick. (This comparison is known to have been a Greek proverb.)

This was not an experience completely like the 'resurrection' appearances at the end of the gospels, because no man appeared. But it was sufficiently like them to entitle Saul of Tarsus to be an *apostolos*, a Greek word which means 'envoy' but which in the New Testament normally has the special meaning of one who has witnessed the 'resurrection' appearances which he then describes to others. Paul himself gives no detailed account of his conversion in any of his letters which have survived. Writing to the Galatians, he simply says: 'God, in his grace, chose me even before I was born, and called me to serve him. And when he decided to reveal his Son to me, so that I might preach the Good News about him to the Gentiles, I did not go to anyone for advice . . .' (1:15-16)

Paul seems to have acknowledged the unique nature of his experience, as when he wrote in his first letter to the Corinthians: 'Last of all he appeared also to me – even though I am like one who was born in a most unusual way.' (15:8) But it was an authentic experience, the proof being contained in the same letter. 'Am I not an apostle? Haven't I seen Jesus our Lord?' (9:1) And 'I have worked harder than all the other apostles'! (15:10)

However, the question whether *Acts* is soberly historical also arises even if we ignore all the references to the 'supernatural'.

Acts includes some disagreeable incidents. It mentions the deaths of Ananias and Sapphira after Peter's curse (5:1-11), the 'quarrel' in the Church with 'Greek-speaking Jews' who said that 'their widows were being neglected in the daily distribution of funds' (6:1-4), the 'sharp argument' between Paul and Barnabas about John Mark (15:39). But it does gloss other difficulties over, and for this reason it has been said not to belong to the real world where (as Paul sadly tells the Philippians, 1:15-17) 'of course some of them preach Christ because they are jealous and quarrelsome' and because they have 'a spirit of selfish ambition'.

For example, we find when we read Paul's letter to the

Galatians (2:11-14) that he had a row with Peter as well as
with Barnabas on another occasion, in Antioch. Both
Peter and Barnabas behaved 'like cowards', Paul tells the
Galatians, by withdrawing from meals with Gentile
Christians because of criticism by 'some men who had
been sent by James' from Jerusalem. Paul had no patience
with Peter. 'I opposed him in public, because he was
clearly wrong.' But there is no reference to this dispute
with Peter in *Acts* – instead, *Acts* claims that Barnabas
was on Paul's side in an argument with some men from
Jerusalem who 'had not, however, received any instructions' to cause trouble (15:2, 24).

Many modern scholars have concluded that much of
Acts is not an account of what actually took place.
According to this view, *Acts* is a work of propaganda,
written as an advertisement for the unity and purity of the
early Church, with idealized characters moving through
idyllic scenes. What is to be our response to this challenge? Are we to say that the author of *Acts* tells the
truth in the sense expressed when in a British court of
law a witness swears to tell 'the truth, the whole truth and
nothing but the truth'? The honest answer is plainly: no.

It so happens that part of *Acts* can be checked from
Paul's surviving correspondence – even if the results of
such a piece of detective work are far from certain. *Acts*
says that the converted Saul or Paul went to Jerusalem
for the *first* time in 9:26-30 (in order to 'join the disciples'),
for the *second* time in 11:30 (in order to deliver money
from the church in Antioch), and for the *third* time in
15:1-31 (in order to 'see the apostles and elders' about
the demand that Gentile Christians must be circumcised). Paul's letter to the Galatians, however, refers to
the first visit ('to get information from Peter'), and adds
that 'fourteen years later I went back to Jerusalem' in
order to discuss 'the gospel message that I preach to the
Gentiles'.

It is difficult to fit these accounts together. If we go by
Paul's own account, then either he has failed to mention
the second visit in *Acts* or it never really took place.
Another problem is that the letter to the Galatians
describes a 'private meeting with the leaders', while *Acts*
tells of a 'long debate' of the 'apostles and elders'. A

third problem is that while *Acts* quotes rules about the admission of the Gentiles, rules which seem to be new and which fill the Church in Antioch with joy, the letter to the Galatians says that 'those who seemed to be leaders – I say this because it makes no difference to me what they were; God does not judge by outward appearances – those leaders, I say, made no new suggestions to me.' In other words, Paul is playing down the significance of the Jerusalem meeting to which *Acts* attaches such importance in chapter 15. It may be, of course, that Paul is here referring to the meeting described in *Acts* in chapter 11, and is writing to the Galatians before the meeting in chapter 15 has taken place – but if so, then we must say that *Acts* underestimates the importance of the chapter 11 meeting!

These problems have been debated in many books, and they can never be solved. They are interesting because they do seem to show that *Acts* cannot be reconciled with Paul's own letters in every detail.

One simpler problem may be dealt with more briefly. In his speech to the Council in Jerusalem a few months after the death of Jesus, the well-known teacher Gamaliel mentions the leaders of two revolts against Rome. 'Some time ago Theudas appeared . . . After this, Judas the Galilean appeared during the time of the census.' (5:36, 37) But according to the Jewish general and historian Josephus, who wrote his *Antiquities* towards the end of the first century, it was Judas who rebelled first, in AD 6 when Quirinius was carrying out a census, while the revolt of Theudas took place some forty years later – about fifteen years after the death of Jesus. The simplest explanation seems to be that *Acts* has got the names muddled.

A number of other minor difficulties could be mentioned. Here is an example. Saul of Tarsus, when he is in Damascus immediately after becoming a Christian, causes so much controversy that he has to escape by being let down over the city wall by night in a basket, and the problem is – from whom is he escaping? *Acts* says that 'the Jews gathered and made plans to kill Saul.' (9:23) But the second letter to the Corinthians recalls that 'the governor under King Aretas placed guards at the city gates to arrest me.' (11:32) The solution may be that Saul is escaping *both* from a mob inside the city *and* from the 'police', stationed at the city gates by the local sheikh.

Even without pausing to study these detailed – it may be thought, trivial – problems, we can see that the author of *Acts* does not tell the whole truth.

For example, he provides an incomplete account of Saul's own tempestuous spiritual journey from that descent in a basket to his venerated grave in Rome as the martyred St Paul. Paul's letter to the Galatians gives us a glimpse of the storm in his mind when he has just been converted – and of his need for privacy to sort things out for himself and perhaps to take his first faltering steps as a Christian preacher (it would seem, without any effects). Paul writes: 'I went at once to Arabia, and then I returned to Damascus. It was three years later that I went to Jerusalem to get information from Peter.' (1:17-18) Chapter 9 of *Acts*, on the other hand, represents the converted Saul as immediately staying with the disciples in Damascus and immediately preaching about Jesus. This ignores the continuing psychological crisis which Saul had to overcome when utterly alone in 'Arabia' (the country and desert district near Damascus, in the modern Syria). Similarly, *Acts* does not give a full account of Paul's later travels and sufferings. Paul tells the Corinthians in his second letter (11:24-5): 'Five times I was given the thirty-nine lashes by the Jews; three times I was whipped by the Romans, and once I was stoned; I have been in three shipwrecks, and once I spent twenty-four hours in the water.' Some, but not all, of these dramatic incidents are recounted in *Acts*.

Paul's two letters to the Thessalonians, almost certainly written from Corinth, show us what problems were created when Christians were so confident that the end of the world was coming quickly that they stopped working. But these problems do not occur in *Acts*. Paul's letters to the Corinthians allow us to enter into his anxiety and depression during his time in Ephesus: he was nearly desperate with worry. And there is a hint of this in *Acts* when Paul bids farewell to the elders of the church in Ephesus and refers to 'many tears' and 'hard times' (20:19). But almost nothing of this bitter mood is reflected in the account of the work in Ephesus in chapter 19 – where instead we read that 'the word of the Lord kept spreading and growing stronger.' Again, Paul's letter to the Romans lets us see how passionately the mature Paul still longs for the conversion of his fellow-Jews to Christ, and how heartfelt is his pride in being a Jew himself – despite his profound criticism of the Jewish religious law. Very little of this emotion comes out in *Acts*. And Paul's letters show what great importance he attached to the collection in the Gentile congregations for the poverty-stricken Christians in Jerusalem and Judea. To Paul, it was a deeply significant expression of Christian unity and love – and (it would seem) taking the money to Jerusalem was the main reason for his very dangerous last visit to the city. In *Acts* this collection is mentioned – but only incidentally, in Paul's speech to Felix (24:17).

It therefore is generally agreed by those who have made a profound study both of *Acts* and of Paul's letters that the author of *Acts* did not have access to those letters when he was writing. Indeed, some scholars wonder how much he would have understood of the letters, if he *had* read them!

One final difficulty may be noticed. There are very few mentions of first-century Christianity in surviving non-Christian sources. This is as we would expect, for probably no one, not even the Christians, then dreamed how quickly the movement described in *Acts* was to become the official religion of the Roman empire. But one result is that only a few of the events described in *Acts* can be connected with non-Christian evidence, or dated certainly. These events can be mentioned quickly.

The story is told of Herod Agrippa's death (12:20-3); this took place in the year 44, but the Jewish historian Josephus tells a different story about it. It is mentioned that 'Emperor Claudius had ordered all the Jews to leave Rome' (18:2). This connects with the statement by the Roman historian Suetonius that the Emperor 'expelled from Rome Jews who were always rioting at the instigation of Chrestus' – a statement which probably shows that Suetonius had heard vaguely of disturbances among the Jews involving the name of Christ. *Acts* says

that 'Gallio was made the Roman governor of Greece'
(18:12); a contemporary inscription found at Delphi
shows that he was governor (of Achaea) in the year 52.
Governor Felix (23:24) is also mentioned by the
historians Tacitus and Josephus. In all, these do not
make a very impressive total of connections with non-
Christian sources.

On the other hand, it is fair to say that the author of
Acts was a man who used his own sources with some care,
so that his book is more than a work of edifying fiction.

How much of *Acts* is based on documents existing
previously? Immense efforts have been put by scholars
into the task of recovering the 'sources' of *Acts*, with
very few agreed results. But we must answer the question
more briefly – and much of our answer must depend on
how we estimate the speeches which together make up
about a third of the book. If we believe that Paul
actually spoke all the speeches attributed to him here,
then we may say that he was never at a loss for a word.
The trouble is that we cannot be sure of this. Perhaps in
real life Paul was not such a superb orator (in his second
letter to the Corinthians, 10:10, he quotes the gibe of his
critics: 'his words are nothing!'). But there is nothing in
these speeches which could not have been spoken by
Paul.

In the early chapters of *Acts* there are long speeches by
Peter (2:14-39 and 3:12-26) and Stephen (7:1-53),
together with important short statements by Peter
(4:8-12 and 5:27-32). These speeches and statements have
been analysed by scholars, and as a result many would
agree that in some of their language and ideas they
reflect the 'primitive' stage of Christianity's development.
For example, Peter says simply that Jesus of Nazareth
was 'a man whose divine mission was clearly shown to
you' (2:22), or God's 'Servant' (3:13). These are modest
titles for Jesus in comparison with the worship which
Christians soon felt compelled to offer to him – develop-
ing Stephen's own cry, 'Lord Jesus, receive my spirit!'
(7:59) We need not believe that *Acts* provides a word-by-
word record of everything that was said; that is highly
unlikely. But it is reasonable to suppose either that some

historical sources are being used here, or (more probably) that with the aid of *some* authentic memoirs the author is making a genuine attempt to think back to the situations of Peter, Stephen, and Paul at different points in the Church's history.

Apart from this question about the speeches, some documents originally distinct seem to have been incorporated into *Acts*. Possible examples are the stories of Stephen's martyrdom (6:8-15, 7:54-60) and Peter's escape (12:1-19). These sources incorporated into *Acts* include some descriptions of travel where the word 'we' is used. The first covers Paul's arrival in Greece (16:10-15). The second covers Paul's last journey to Jerusalem (beginning at 20:5) and his voyage to Rome (beginning at 27:1). These parts of *Acts* are sometimes called 'travel diaries', which may be an exaggeration, for they may have been written some time after the events being described, so that errors may have crept in through a faulty memory, and touches may have been added to improve the dramatic effect. But there is no reason why these parts should refer to 'us', and the rest of *Acts* to 'they', if the whole of *Acts* is imaginative.

Nor is there any reason why so many placenames and other details should be mentioned in *Acts*, if the only aim is to paint a pretty picture. One example is a mention of a haircut: 'Before sailing he made a vow in Cenchreae and had his head shaved.' (18:18)

It is also instructive to watch how careful *Acts* is to get details such as the titles and names of officials right. There were various ranks in various parts of the Roman empire, and the Greek terms in *Acts* are right in every case. *Acts* distinguishes between the 'governor' or *anthupatos* (in Latin, *proconsul*) Sergius Paulus in Cyprus (13:7), the 'Roman officials' or *strategoi* in Philippi (16:20), the 'city authorities' or *politarchai* in Thessalonica (17:6), the 'meeting of the Areopagus' in Athens (17:19), the 'governor' Gallio (18:12), the 'provincial authorities' or *Asiarchoi* in Ephesus (19:31), the *hegemon* (in Latin, *procurator*) Felix and his successor Porcius Festus (23:24, 24:27), and Publius the 'chief' or *protos* (in Latin, *primus*) in Malta (28:7).

The upshot seems to be that *Acts* is the work of an

author who tends not to draw attention to quarrels, who can make small mistakes, and who has no wish to probe deeply into theology or psychology. And, as we saw earlier, it is a book full of the wonders of the 'supernatural'. But it is also the work of an author who cares about political titles and other facts which belong to the same world as handkerchiefs.

Fortunately, its opening supplies the key to its purpose. *Acts* is dedicated to Theophilus, and begins: 'In my first book I wrote about all the things that Jesus did and taught . . .' At once we see that this is a sequel to the third gospel. That gospel is also dedicated to Theophilus, and it begins: 'Because I have carefully studied all these matters from their beginning, I thought it good to write an orderly account for you. I do this so that you will know the full truth of all those matters which you have been taught.'

Who was Theophilus? No one knows. The name means in Greek 'Lover of God', so it is possible that the use of the name here means that the two volumes are dedicated to all who love God. But real people did have this name, and probably there was some important person called Theophilus. Normally in the first century when a book was dedicated to someone, that person was expected to be a patron, rewarding the author and arranging for copies to be made of his book (which was, of course, hand-written, not printed). But it sounds as if Theophilus was thought to have sincerely religious motives for wanting the 'full truth' about Jesus and the first Christians. He may have been a sympathetic inquirer, perhaps a Roman official. But it sounds as if he had already been taught enough to become a Christian – and already knew enough about Christianity and its background not to be completely puzzled or put off by (for example) frequent Old Testament quotations. What we do know is that the author by writing this kind of dedication implied that he was fitting into the conventions of first-century literature. It was quite normal to dedicate a book like this, and to promise that it would tell the truth.

The identity of the author of these two volumes is not

mentioned in the texts which have come down to us, although it may have been included in the titles given to the two books (or rather, scrolls) originally. In the evidence which survives from the second Christian century (the Muratorian Canon and a work against heretics by Irenaeus, Bishop of Lyons – also the *Anti-Marcionite Prologues*, if these *are* second-century), the author is named as Luke, and there is no good reason to contradict this. Nor is there any good reason to doubt that the man who wrote the 'we' sections also wrote, or compiled, the rest of *Acts*.

But who was Luke? *Acts* is silent. The letter to the Colossians refers to several Gentile Christians and among them 'Luke, our dear doctor' (4:11, 14). The second letter to Timothy says that 'only Luke is with me.' (4:11) If these letters, or these bits of them, are genuinely by Paul, then we know as much about Luke as we do about most people who are mentioned in *Acts*. If they are not by Paul, they may still preserve reliable information about Luke. These references fit in with the impression left by *Acts* that its author was Paul's fellow-traveller. They also fit in with the special interest taken (both in the third gospel and in *Acts*) in healing – although the attempt to find a technical medical vocabulary in these books is not convincing. But we cannot be certain where Luke came from, or how he became a Christian. If he was the author of the 'we' sections, he joined Paul at Troas (16:10) and was left behind to organize the new church in Philippi (16:16), later rejoining Paul (20:6) and staying with him through his dangers and trials. He writes good conversational Greek. When he quotes the Old Testament, he uses the Greek translation (the Septuagint) – even in the course of speeches by Simon Peter, and even in the mouth of James the brother of Jesus (15:16-18)! As a geographer he seems better equipped to describe Asia Minor than Palestine.

We feel we know his character. His whole attitude in his gospel and in *Acts* shows that he was a sensitive and compassionate man. It is to him that we owe the preservation of the parables of the good Samaritan and the good father (otherwise called the parable of the prodigal son).

Some of the artistry in those brilliant short stories – for example, their economy in words – seems to be due to Luke's own rare gifts as a writer (although Jesus was no mean story-teller himself!). And Luke responded deep down to the idea of a journey. Not only is *Acts* a travel book. The whole of the central section of Luke's gospel (9:51-19:27) is presented in the setting of a long journey by Jesus, before the great story of the entry into Jerusalem and eternal glory (19:28-24:53). But as he travelled, Luke was interested in people rather than scenery. (The tradition that he was a painter has made him the patron saint of painters, but it is no earlier than the eighth century.) The different places are noted briefly, but only as the background to the drama that matters, which is meeting new people. On the other hand, Luke was no psychologist. He preferred to hint at characters by showing them in action. He was also no philosopher; he told stories.

This does not mean, however, that he was a good-hearted, simple-minded country doctor without any ideas of his own. On the contrary, modern scholars have devoted much study to the 'theology' of Luke. Some of them have classed him as the most influential theologian in the whole of the New Testament – because his understanding of Christianity, expressed as it so often was in delightful pictures and stories, has in practice influenced the Church more than the intellectual and difficult theologies of Paul and John. But this is going too far.

Some less reliable, although not impossible, traditions may be mentioned. Many early manuscripts of *Acts* (not accepted as the basis of Today's English Version) include a sentence mentioning 'we' in Antioch (11:28). One ancient document (*The Anti-Marcionite Prologues*) says that Luke lived until the age of 84. According to Eusebius at the beginning of the fourth century, he came from Antioch, wrote his gospel in Greece, and had been identified (by the Christian philosopher Origen) with 'the brother who is highly respected in all the churches for his work in preaching the gospel', mentioned in Paul's second letter to the Corinthians (8:18).

We do not know when *Acts* was written or published.

The first definite quotation from it occurs in the *Apology* of Justin Martyr, written about the middle of the second century. Earlier Christian writings may refer to it, but not clearly enough to provide proof. Mainly because of the differences between *Acts* and Paul's letters, some scholars conclude that the author of *Acts* cannot have known Paul well, and they believe that *Acts* was written in the second Christian century. But this is to exaggerate the problems about the accuracy of *Acts*. It would have been perfectly possible for Luke to have been the 'dear doctor' and the fellow-traveller of Paul over considerable periods without understanding completely either his life or his theology. At the other extreme, some scholars argue that *Acts* must have been written before AD 64, because that is the traditional date (approximately) of the martyrdoms of Peter and Paul – which are not mentioned in *Acts*. Most readers of the statements that Paul expected death (20:38, 21:13) will think it probable that Paul was dead when *Acts* was completed.

On the whole, the probability is that Acts was completed at some time between 70 and 90. We say 'completed', although there are various small examples of clumsiness remaining in the Greek text and suggesting that there was never a final revision. There is, in fact, some doubt about whether a number of sentences found in some manuscripts belonged to *Acts* as it left its author's hand; a few of these are printed in Today's English Version in square brackets (notably 8:37).

The reasons why this period 70-90 is thought probable by most scholars are chiefly psychological. Around the year 95, the Emperor Domitian launched a savage persecution against the Christian Church. It is to this terrible time that the last book in the New Testament, *The Revelation to John*, belongs. But the atmosphere in *Acts* is much calmer, and the Roman officials are usually treated with a polite respect. That suggests the year 90 as the latest. Another argument which has the same result depends on the fact that *Acts* is not based on the letters of Paul – which seem to have been published as a collection in about 90.

The year 70 is thought to be the earliest because if *Acts* was published some years after the deaths of Peter and

Paul in 64 (?), and the fall of Jerusalem in 70, then it is easier to understand the calm tone of Luke's account of the relations between these two apostles, and between them and James and the elders of the church in Jerusalem. If Luke completed his book some years after 70, he would view all the controversies in perspective – for when he wrote Peter and Paul were both in the noble army of martyrs, and Jerusalem was in ruins, its temple a heap of rubble, its Christians scattered. At that date, the battles looked very different from the view which Paul took when he wrote his front-line despatch to the Galatians twenty or thirty years before. In the 70s or later, death and destruction had settled at least some of the problems – leaving, however, memories of a golden age. And by then, it was impossible to discover or to check all the details of far-off events. Someone writing in Italy, Greece or Turkey during the 1970s or 1980s could not expect to be completely accurate about events in Palestine in the 1930s or 1950s – not even with the aid of newspapers and other modern aids to the historian.

Another argument for a date after the fall of Jerusalem is that Luke's gospel prophesies this in some detail (21:20-4) – which suggests to many scholars that the gospel, with *Acts* as its sequel, was written after 70. But it may be reckoned a stronger argument that Mark's gospel is generally believed to have been written after Peter's death in 64 (?) – and that Luke's gospel is almost certainly based in part on Mark's.

Why, then, are the deaths of Peter and Paul in Rome during the terrible persecution under Nero (when Christians were used as living torches) not used as the climax of *Acts*? No one knows for certain. It is possible that Luke wrote an ending to *Acts* which has perished, or even a lost third volume covering the last years of Paul's life. But most scholars now believe that the present ending to *Acts* is deliberate. 'For two years' Paul in Rome 'preached about the Kingdom of God and taught about the Lord Jesus Christ, speaking with all boldness and freedom.' (28:30, 31) What a triumphant note to strike in a story which began in a manger in Bethlehem, where 'there was no room for them to stay in the inn' (*Luke* 2:7)! For the Saviour born in Bethlehem is the true hero of *Acts*, and no description of his apostles' deaths must be allowed to detract from the centrality of the death and victory of Jesus. This may well have been Luke's attitude.

And here may be the explanation of two of the most puzzling features of *Acts*. Why does Luke take so long to tell us about Paul's sufferings and speeches after his arrest in Jerusalem? This material occupies the space from the middle of chapter 21 to the end of chapter 26, and it seems to hold up the action. And why is so much more space sacrificed to Paul's voyage to Rome, the storm at sea, and the shipwreck, in the long chapter 27? There are so many things about the early Church we should like to know – and here Luke goes on about the winds and the waves! The explanation may be that in Luke's design these chapters are the equivalent of his description in his gospel of the arrest, trial, and agony of Jesus himself. Here the Church – born or reborn on the first Whitsunday as Jesus was born on the first Christmas Day, tested as Jesus was, teaching and healing as Jesus did, almost always on the move like Jesus – passed through its equivalent of Good Friday.

If Luke was one of those involved in the shipwreck on Malta, it would be very interesting to know exactly how 'we all got safely ashore.' (27:44) Was Luke one of those who could swim, or was he among the others who held 'on to the planks or to some broken pieces of the ship'?

It is not idle curiosity that makes us ask. For if Luke had made notes about his own travels, about the life of Jesus, and about the history of the apostles, those notes may have been lost in the shipwreck. On the other hand, the precious bundle may have been rescued. If we knew this, we could know whether or not the gospel and *Acts* use material written down during Luke's travels with Paul, and during the 'two years' which he seems to have passed in Caesarea when Paul was in prison there (24:27). Caesarea was a shining new town by the sea, and the Roman headquarters in Palestine. Before going to Jerusalem, Paul had stayed there, in the house of Philip the evangelist (21:8). If Luke spent two years in that house, he would have had many opportunities to gather information.

What we can know for sure is that the third gospel and

Acts together form two volumes of almost exactly the same length – perhaps the first should be called *The Acts of Jesus*. Together they constitute more than a quarter of the New Testament. The dedication of these books to Theophilus is only one reflection of the fact that the books are written in a civilized and colourful way, with much the same sort of style as a number of other history books of the same century. We also know that both the gospel and *Acts* present Christianity in a most attractive light. These books are beautifully written, and they are written about good people.

Both Jesus and the apostles are described as coming into conflict with the narrow-minded and prejudiced Jewish religious authorities, and mobs can be stirred up against the apostles, but the Roman authorities are said to have been unwilling to condemn either Jesus or his followers. Pilate says repeatedly to the chief priests and the crowds that Jesus is innocent. 'I find no reason to condemn this man.' (*Luke* 23:4) The first Roman official whom Paul meets as a missionary, Sergius Paulus, in Cyprus (whose name has been found on an inscription in Rome), becomes a Christian (13:12). Gallio, the Roman governor in Corinth (and the brother of the philosopher Seneca, Nero's prime minister), dismisses the Jews' charges against Paul as 'an argument about words and names and your own law' (18:15). Chapter 23 carefully describes how Paul is rescued by the Roman army from a mob in Jerusalem. King Agrippa and Festus conclude: 'This man has not done anything for which he should die or be put in prison.' (26:31) And Paul sums up his defence: 'I have done nothing wrong against the Law of the Jews, or the temple, or the Roman Emperor.' (25:8) The whole tone of *Acts* suggests that, to the fair-minded, Christianity must be innocent.

This is fascinating. Whether or not Jesus and Paul really were as non-controversial as Luke makes out, when *Acts* was written Christianity was often thought to be an enemy of society. Jesus, Peter, and Paul had all been executed because they had been judged to be in some sense rebels. In his gospel Luke had to admit that Pontius Pilate had fixed above Jesus the charge of rebellion on which he was being crucified: 'This is the King of the

Jews.' (23:38) In *Acts* Luke had to admit that soon after his arrival in Europe Paul was being accused of 'breaking the laws of the Emperor, saying that there is another king, by the name of Jesus' (17:7) – and that in Jerusalem Paul was confused for a time with 'that Egyptian fellow' who had been a notorious leader of terrorists (21:38). The reputation of encouraging rebellion was a very dangerous one to have in the Roman empire. And the one way of clearing their reputation – a little incense offered in sacrifice to a statue of the divine Emperor – was rejected by the Christians. Nor did the Christians' reputation stand high among those not particularly interested in questions about their political loyalty. Not only did most of the Jews reject with indignation the claims made about Jesus. Many of the Gentiles believed stories that the Christians were a secret society (because they met in private), spoilsports (because they would not attend dinner parties where prayers might be said to the gods and meat served which had been sacrificed in a temple), atheists (because they would not join in the 'harmless' convention of sacrificing to the gods in the course of many social activities), hypocrites who indulged in incest and orgies (because they spoke of 'brothers' and 'sisters' loving each other in 'love feasts'), and cannibals (because they ate a 'body' and drank 'blood'). The Emperor, Nero, had made the Christians the scapegoats who were blamed for everything that went wrong – just as Hitler was to treat the Jews in Germany.

Whoever wrote the third gospel and *Acts*, and whatever material he used, he was an author who boldly and confidently dedicated all his skills to the task of showing Theophilus that Christianity deserved not persecution but love. And he did this not by saying, 'I will argue against Christianity's critics' – but by saying, 'I will tell you the history.'

In the first century no historian was expected to write the kind of book we expect from professional historians today. He enjoyed a freedom which nowadays we do not allow if a history book is to be taken seriously. He was expected to write a readable and enjoyable book, dramatizing events, leaving out the dull bits, reporting legends and other good stories without being too worried

about their accuracy, putting in his own guesses where
his knowledge ran out, and adding his own interpreta-
tions, particularly in the form of speeches made by the
chief characters at key points. This was not only true of
historical writers with a religious (?) motivation such as
Josephus the Jewish historian. It was also true of
immortally great historians of Greece and Rome such as
Herodotus, Thucydides, Livy, and Tacitus. On the other
hand, an historian was *not* expected to write a book
which had no connection with what really happened. He
was *not* writing for people who were so bemused with
fantasies that they would not recognize a fact when they
saw one. People assumed that he would provide a mixture
of fact, drama, and interpretation – not pure fiction.
There were works of fiction circulating in the first
century (or soon after) which entertained or edified people
with stories about Jesus and the Christians. We know
this both from Luke's introductory reference to the
'many' who had attempted to write gospels before him,
and from the 'apocryphal' gospels and the 'apocryphal'
narratives about the apostles which have survived. The
atmosphere in these apocryphal gospels and apocryphal
acts is an atmosphere of fantasy.

The author of *Acts* wrote a history of the Christians
as 'history' was then understood. So far as we know, he
was the pioneer in this – the very first Christian historian.
And thanks to his enterprise, we have not only some good
stories but also some evidence about the first Christian
generation.

3. THE GOOD NEWS

In our time many people ask the question: how can the Christian message be made powerful and relevant? And this was precisely the question which the first Christian generation had to face, so soon after the foundation of the Church. Jesus and his first followers were almost all Jews. Yet most Jews rejected the claims about Jesus, and forced Christians to argue. And beyond Judaism there were millions of Gentiles who were not familiar with the Jewish phrases which Jesus and his first followers had used constantly: phrases such as 'Kingdom of God' and 'Son of Man'. For this wider world, Christianity had to be translated into a new language. It seems reasonable to expect the first Christian generation to have something to teach us about the method by which the 'Good News' can be presented afresh – while not betraying its permanent truth or diluting its inner essence merely in order to be fashionable.

First, however, we should note that everything was not made easy for these early Christians. Even when it was (so to speak) hot from the oven, Christianity was not immediately seen to be the spiritual food for which the world was hungry.

The first half of *Acts* tells us of some remarkable conversions, but the hard statistics would seem to be that the Christian Church had only a few thousand members before Paul at last began his mission to the Gentiles in Pisidian Antioch (13:46). We do not know when this was, but a date around the year 45 is probable – and this was fifteen years or so after the crucifixion of Jesus and a dozen years or so after Paul's own conversion. According to *Acts*, Paul and Barnabas avoided optimism; their teaching was that 'we must pass through many troubles to enter the Kingdom of God.' (14:22) And Paul's farewell speech after about a dozen years of work in Asia Minor and Greece strikes a sombre note: 'I only know that in every city the Holy Spirit has warned me that prison and troubles wait for me.' (20:23)

Acts shows that even the genius Paul could not make

himself understood by a hostile audience. In every synagogue where he preached while a Christian, he failed to impress most of the congregation. And because he grew to expect rejection, he is shown as often not even attempting a full statement of the Christian message.

Thus in Athens he at first conveys the impression that he is discussing two 'foreign gods' when he is preaching 'about Jesus and the resurrection' (17:18) – but the speech which is attributed to him as his great statement to the intellectuals goes to the opposite extreme of never once naming Jesus. When he is being examined by the Council in Jerusalem, he loses his temper with the High Priest and has to apologize (23:5) – and his only defence of his position is to appeal to his fellow-Pharisees by claiming: 'I am on trial here because I hope that the dead will rise to life!' (23:6) This is a good dodge in a debate, but as a statement of Christianity it is neither comprehensive nor effective.

Later, when he appears before the Roman Governor Felix in Caesarea, he finds himself addressing an official 'who was well informed about the Way' (24:22) – a change from Gallio, the Governor in Corinth, who was so bored by questions about the Jewish religion that even an assault on one of the witnesses in Paul's trial there 'did not bother Gallio a bit' (18:17). But Paul's hopes of Felix failed for a sordid reason. Felix was accompanied by his wife Drusilla, who was Jewish. She was the daughter of 'King Herod', Agrippa I, and the sister of King Agrippa II – and she was the wife of Azizus, King of Emesa. Felix had seduced her, to make her his third wife. No wonder that he interrupted Paul ('I will call you again when I get the chance') when Paul 'went on discussing about goodness, self-control, and the coming Day of Judgment' (24:25)!

On the evidence of *Acts*, it is just not true that the first Christians had only to speak in order to convert. And we ought to remember these difficulties experienced by the first Christian generation when we consider our own problems. For we are entitled to claim that the problems we face are as great as any met in *Acts* – if not greater.

The Christians in the period of *Acts* did not have to cope with an atmosphere of secular materialism. On the contrary, the first Christian generation had the advantage of finding an interest in religion everywhere. That is obviously true of Jewish life in Palestine. Belief in God, the willingness to obey and worship him, and a stable family life could all be taken for granted. What needed to be criticized was not atheism, or slackness, or gross immorality – but religious hypocrisy. It is certain and immensely significant that both Jesus and Paul remained loyal Jews in many ways, for although they were revolutionaries they could build on the Jewish religious tradition. It comes as no surprise to find Paul speaking to a crowd in Jerusalem in Hebrew – speaking as one who had been 'brought up here in Jerusalem' and who had seen Jesus in a vision 'while I was praying in the temple' (22:3, 17). The surprise is that this vision is not mentioned elsewhere!

The same atmosphere of strong religion seems to exist wherever the first Christians go in *Acts*. Not merely are there Jews dispersed around the Mediterranean and meeting faithfully in 'synagogues' in place after place. On the first Saturday which Paul spent in Europe he found himself in Philippi, lodging in a Gentile house where the exact address of the synagogue was not known. But Paul and his companions were certain that there must be a Jewish synagogue in this Roman town. 'On the Sabbath day we went out of the city to the riverside, where we thought there would be a Jewish place for prayer.' (16:13) Frequently in *Acts* Paul relies on the synagogue for his first contacts in a strange place.

In the world depicted in *Acts*, piety extended far beyond the ranks of the Jews and their converts, the 'proselytes'. Many pagans were associated closely with the Jews and were known as 'God-fearers'. For example, Captain Cornelius of the Italian Regiment 'was a religious man; he and his whole family worshipped God' (10:2). And many pagans were religious in their own way. Paul's speech can begin: 'Men of Athens! I see that in every way you are very religious . . .' (17:22) A city clerk calms passions with another compliment: 'Men of Ephesus! . . . Everyone knows that the city of Ephesus is the keeper of the temple of the great Artemis and of the sacred stone that fell down from heaven.' (19:35)

But these are not the conditions familiar to most modern readers of *Acts*. Even if they can find many army officers noted with their whole families for their piety, modern readers will not come across many intellectuals who would take it as a compliment to be called 'very religious'. In the modern equivalent of Ephesus the public would probably take more pride in the local football team than in the local temple, and would deposit the 'sacred stone' in the local museum as a meteorite. Local loyalty does not often take such a loudly religious form as when 'they all shouted together the same thing for two hours: "Great is Artemis of Ephesus!" ' (19:34)

So *Acts*, although it is on the whole a success story, shows us that the early Church's success was not always rapid or complete – and was not in circles which rejected religion. It is important for us to realize just how ironic King Agrippa was being when he taunted Paul: 'In this short time do you think you will make me a Christian?' (26:28) This is important, for it reminds us that when we grapple with our twentieth-century difficulties we need not have the depressing feeling that the first Christians would have done miraculously better if they had been in our situation.

On the other hand, *Acts* is not irrelevant to Christianity's tasks and hopes in the twentieth-century crisis of religious belief. We should not fail to notice one reason why the Church in the age of *Acts* was as successful as it was. Its message seemed to some to be the answer to the problem created by the spiritual crisis of the first century. On the surface, first-century religion flourished. But in their hearts many people seem to have grown deeply dissatisfied with their religious traditions. Indeed, some of the most sensitive people then alive were frankly disgusted.

Acts contains several pointers to this religious crisis. Luke, who often seems remote from our age of science because of the readiness with which he tells stories of miracles and angels, adopts a tone of cool irony towards the superstitions of the people of Malta. 'The natives saw the snake hanging on Paul's hand and said to one another, "This man must be a murderer, but Fate will not let him live . . ." But Paul shook the snake off . . . and . . . they changed their minds and said, "He is a god!" ' (28:4-6) He also records with satisfaction that in Ephesus 'many of those who had practised magic' burned their very expensive books on becoming Christians (19:18-20). And he represents Paul as being hotly indignant, instead of touristically admiring, when he saw the temples of Athens: 'he was greatly upset when he noticed how full of idols the city was.' (17:16) No doubt Paul was even more hostile towards the religion of Ephesus, which is known to have involved the ritual use of prostitutes in the temple of the many-breasted fertility goddess, as well as the exploitation of the souvenir trade by the silversmiths.

Not only Christians and Jews were unable to accept the paganism established in the first century. We are often reminded in *Acts* how many Gentiles had been converted to Judaism, which because of its worship of only one God and its high moral standards was very attractive in an age of spiritual hunger. Pagans themselves were dissatisfied. *Acts* is being true to first-century life when it suggests that at least some Athenians really did worship not idols but 'an Unknown God' (although no altar has been discovered with that inscription), that it was easy for 'this fellow Paul' to persuade many Ephesians that 'gods made by men are not gods at all', and that the city clerk of Ephesus was more interested in preserving law and order than in the defence of the city's religion (11:23; 19:26, 35-41). There is abundant evidence surviving from this period that many thoughtful people had lost interest in the official religion of temples and priests. This religion was supported mainly because it was good for law and order – and for trade.

All this indicates that the foundations of paganism were not so strong as they seemed to be. There was also an undercurrent of radical criticism within the Jewish religion, as may be seen particularly in chapter 7 of *Acts*. This chapter gives the speech by Stephen, the first Christian martyr.

Stephen is not supposed to be a preacher at all. He is one

of the seven 'helpers' put in charge of the finances of the
Church (6:1-6). And he is not a hundred per cent accurate
in his knowledge of the Old Testament, although he
delivers this short (but not so short!) history of Israel to a
formidable audience, the priests' council in Jerusalem.

He makes careless mistakes, most of which we know
from other evidence were commonly made by Greek-
speaking Jews who relied on the Septuagint, the Old Testament translated into Greek. Stephen begins: 'Brothers
and fathers! Listen to me! The God of glory appeared
to our ancestor Abraham while he was living in Mesopotamia . . .' But that is a mistake. According to the
original Hebrew of *Genesis* (12:6-7), God appeared to
Abraham in Shechem in Canaan. Stephen does mention
Shechem: he refers to Abraham's grave there (7:16).
Unfortunately, however, *Genesis* (23:19, 25:9) says that
Abraham was buried in Hebron. It is understandable
that many who begin reading this chapter are tempted to
skip over it, reckoning it nothing more than a second-
rate sermon. Even scholars have found it boring or
puzzling. But despite its lack of polish, its purpose is
clear. It is a root-and-branch protest against traditional
religion, and the contempt it shows for detailed accuracy
leads into the dismissal of everything represented by the
priests.

Its theme is that the religion of these Jewish priests is
the enemy of the truth. 'How stubborn you are! How
heathen your hearts, how deaf you are to God's message!
You are just like your ancestors: you too have always
resisted the Holy Spirit! Was there any prophet that your
ancestors did not persecute? . . . And now you have
betrayed and murdered him' – Jesus (7:51-2). In accordance with this theme, Stephen shouts out that Moses, the
man of God, was rejected by Israel (7:35) – and that the
temple, said to be the Lord's own house, was rejected by
God (7:48).

It is an extraordinary speech to find in *Acts* – and not
only because it is so long. Why is it there? Because it
impressed Saul of Tarsus? But nowhere in *Acts* (or in his
letters) does Paul reject the Jewish religion with the
ruthlessness of Stephen. Because it sums up the Old
Testament for Gentile readers of *Acts*? But it makes a

very slap-dash summary. Because it represents Luke's own position? But we have seen elsewhere in his writing that Luke shows himself to be a man of peace. The nearest he comes to echoing Stephen's totally negative view in *Acts* is when he quotes Peter as describing the Law of Moses as 'a load . . . which neither our ancestors nor we ourselves were able to carry' (15:10). In his gospel he quotes Jesus as denouncing the arrogance and hypocrisy of the teachers of the Law (*Luke* 11:37-12:3). These attacks are, however, not so thorough as Stephen's, and they should be seen in perspective. In the early chapters of Luke's gospel a sensitively poetic use is made of the Old Testament and the boy Jesus is welcomed into the Jerusalem temple, where he later listens eagerly to the Jewish teachers. In the early chapters of *Acts* 'the people' in Jerusalem speak highly of the apostles and their group (5:13). In the later chapters, Paul is determined to go as a pilgrim to Jerusalem and to its temple. Our abiding impression is that Luke, although he probably spent only a few weeks in the city, shared Jesus's own love for it and its temple – the love so memorably expressed: 'O Jerusalem, Jerusalem! . . . How many times I wanted to put my arms round all your people, just as a hen gathers her chicks under her wings . . . !' (*Luke* 13:34)

The explanation seems to be that Luke wishes to show us the religious crisis. At a very early stage Christianity included in its ranks men who were fiercely impatient with the whole religious tradition which they had inherited. Conventional religion – even Judaism as it was practised in the Holy City – stank in their nostrils. And whatever the fury that might result, as when 'the members of the Council . . . ground their teeth at him in anger' (7:54), such radicals were not guilty. They were seeking a purer reality – and finding it. They were worshipping an unknown God – now known. 'Stephen, full of the Holy Spirit, looked up to heaven and saw God's glory, and Jesus standing . . .' (7:55) Standing! It is more usual to find the glorified Lord Jesus spoken of as 'seated at the right hand of God'. But here Jesus *stands* – in welcome to the rebel.

In order that I may complete my mission and finish the

work that the Lord Jesus gave me to do, which is to declare the Good News of the grace of God.' This comes in *Acts* (20:24), but it might equally well have come from one of Paul's letters. It sums up the motivation not only of Paul but of many others whom we meet in *Acts*. Their task was derived from Jesus himself – historical and living, crucified and crowned. It was not to express themselves, to build up their own power or prestige. It was not even to extend the influence of the Church. It was simply to 'finish the work that the Lord Jesus gave me to do'. And the work consisting of declaring the 'Good News'. It was not to announce bad news, to utter warnings, to criticize and denounce. It was not even to offer good advice, to teach wise philósophy or psychology or politics or economics. It was simply to be 'witnesses' (1:18) – to announce facts, facts which must produce joy. And the 'Good News' was itself not philosophical, psychological, political or economic. It was news about God, and about his 'grace'. That was the heart of Christianity for this first Christian generation. And we need only add that those who knew that Christianity had this heart did not need to be exhorted about their duty to evangelize. As Peter and John exclaim in *Acts*: 'we cannot stop speaking of what we ourselves have seen and heard.' (4:20) Those who had really heard the 'Good News' were bursting with it.

When we ask how the 'Good News' or Gospel is expressed in *Acts*, we naturally expect it to be a message about Jesus. But we are immediately faced by a problem, for the life and teaching of Jesus are not described at all fully in the speeches and sermons in *Acts*.

We have already noted that Paul's speech in Athens never names Jesus, but the same is true of Stephen's speech in Jerusalem. The five sermons of Peter mention the life and teaching of Jesus only as leading up to his death and resurrection (2:22-4, 3:13-15, 4:10, 5:30, 10:37-40). Paul's sermon in Pisidian Antioch (13:23-30) is similar. The only words of Jesus directly quoted by Paul in *Acts* are: 'There is more happiness in giving than in receiving.' (20:35) Paul's surviving letters have the same character, and all this has led many scholars to argue that the religion of the early Christians was not greatly interested in the historical figure of Jesus of Nazareth. It is suggested that the teaching *of* Jesus dropped out of the picture, to be replaced by teaching *about* Jesus. It is also suggested that this teaching about Jesus was a kind of mysticism; Christians could be united in spirit with this divine Saviour and could live 'in Christ' – in much the same way that members of pagan cults could be united with *their* mythical saviours. The word 'Saviour' or 'salvation' occurs sixteen times in *Acts*.

We cannot deal fully with Paul's attitude. Discussing that must depend on Paul's letters and on books about them. But at least it is certain that Paul did present the person-to-person appeal of Jesus, particularly of the death of Jesus. The elders of the church in Ephesus are told in *Acts*: 'Be shepherds of the church of God, which he made his own through the death of his own son.' (20:28) That brief reference to the personal appeal of the crucified Jesus is amplified many times in Paul's letters. This speech to the elders also refers to the central theme in the teaching of Jesus, the 'Kingdom of God' (20:25). Admittedly this phrase, which occurs eight times in *Acts*, is not so prominent in Paul's letters, but the best explanation is that it is a Jewish phrase and that the letters were written mainly to Gentiles. The idea behind the phrase – God triumphing and being obeyed – is thoroughly Pauline.

We can also say with confidence that the attitude of the author of *Acts*, who is responsible for the final writing or editing of all these speeches or sermons (whatever sources he may have used), can be known – and it is complete nonsense to suggest that the author of *Acts* has little interest in the life and teaching of Jesus.

The reason why we can say this with confidence is perfectly simple. The man who wrote *Acts* also wrote Luke's gospel! It is certain that he was fascinated by the parables, by the healings and (as he puts it in the very first sentence of *Acts*) by 'all the things that Jesus did and taught'. The truth must be that what we read as the speeches or sermons in *Acts* are really only outlines of what was said – or of what was thought by the author of *Acts* to have been typical Christian preaching. In the actual presentation of the Christian message, a great deal of time must have been spent in explaining who Jesus was, as when Philip told the Ethiopian 'the Good News about Jesus' (8:35). In no other way can the name of Jesus have been made attractive to people who had never heard of him – or who, if they had heard of him, would have regarded him as an executed criminal.

If we are to recapture the original message of Christianity, we must picture Christian preachers telling again and again the story of the Saviour's life as a man, and retelling the stories which Jesus told. When Christianity was presented to outsiders, the emphasis would be on the way in which Jesus met outsiders, spreading faith, peace, joy, and health. Jesus was – this is the magnificently simple phrase in *Acts* (3:15) – 'the one who leads men to life'. When Christianity was taught to inquirers, the emphasis would be on the teaching of Jesus about God, God's Kingdom and God's demands – all leading into the forgiveness of sins after repentance, and into baptism 'in the name of Jesus'. When Christians met for worship, the emphasis would be on how Jesus had laid down his life for his friends – and enemies; on this, and on the victory and continuing life of Jesus, to be experienced within that act of worship. For the stories of the crucifixion and resurrection of Jesus must have been told innumerable times in Christian worship before any one of the gospels was written, and the rest of the material which we can now read in the gospels must have been shaped out of a mass of Christian talking.

A theological genius such as Paul was no doubt expected to present his own original interpretation – even if 'as Paul kept on talking . . . a young man named Eutychus got sleepier and sleepier' (20:7-9)! But a more routine teacher such as Luke himself was more likely to concentrate on telling people about Jesus. Surely, his own experience in preaching and teaching over many years was what encouraged Luke to find out more and more historical facts and eventually to write his two books. He paid little attention to systematic theology (it is significant that the phrase 'Son of God' occurs only once in *Acts*: 9:20). He had discovered what kept people awake.

However, what kept the first Christian teachers at such a pitch of excitement, and what kept their hearers awake, was not merely speaking about Jesus as if he had been a dead philosopher or prophet. And it was no dry-as-dust repetition of stories about Jesus. On the contrary, the message of *Acts* is about the *living* Jesus. The Roman official Festus sums it up accurately. Christianity, he observes, is 'about a man named Jesus, who has died; but Paul claims that he is alive' (25:19).

The great fact is shouted in Peter's first sermon: 'God has raised this very Jesus from the dead, and we are all witnesses to this fact . . . and what you now see and hear is his gift that he has poured out on us.' (2:32-3) Jesus lives! And Jesus gives! The message of *Acts* is that, just as God had poured out on Jesus 'the Holy Spirit and power' (10:38), so the same Holy Spirit can now be experienced by Christians – with the same power, so that all would praise God's greatness (10:46). When Christian teachers told stories about Jesus, they had to confess that while Jesus had lived physically among men, his followers (including Peter) had often failed to understand him. In the end, all (including Peter) had betrayed or deserted him. But now, after the death and victory of Jesus, a new power had been released. The Christian message was the promise of power – given by people filled with power. They showed this power by their new boldness, and by their loyalty which was not afraid of death. Inevitably people all over the Roman world asked with the priests in Jerusalem: 'How did you do this? What power do you have?' (4:7)

Acts confesses clearly that Christians who claim to be full of the Holy Spirit may still make mistakes. For example, when Paul is on his last journey to Jerusalem he stays with some Christians in the port of Tyre, and he is warned by them: 'By the power of the Spirit they told Paul not to go to Jerusalem.' But Paul rejects their warning: 'when our time with them was over, we left and went on our way.' (21:4, 5) And the author of *Acts* clearly believes that it turned out to be God's will that Paul should go to Jerusalem – and Rome.

Acts also shows that the Christians at that early stage had not developed the Trinitarian doctrine that God is three Persons: Father, Son, and Holy Spirit. It seemed at first both natural and sufficient to think of the Holy

Spirit very simply, as God's gift – which may suggest to readers familiar with Trinitarian orthodoxy that these early Christians made the mistake of thinking of the Holy Spirit as a thing, rather than as a Person. Such readers may also conclude that *Acts* makes the mistake of confusing the Persons of the Trinity, as when one sentence refers to 'the Holy Spirit' and the next sentence to 'the Spirit of Jesus' (16:6, 7). But if the later doctrine is not there, the facts are there! These early Christians were on the way to being compelled to acknowledge that God discloses himself in three modes of being. The new power greater than themselves and greater than their understanding was life like wind, or fire. It was straight from God through Jesus – but it was *new* life, not the life of God experienced through nature or through history, not the life of God embodied in the life of Jesus. People who had this experience were being driven to worship God as Father, Son, and Spirit.

One reason why these Christians were so sure about this was that the Spirit did *not* always echo their own wishes. On the contrary, 'the Holy Spirit did not let them preach the message in the province of Asia' when they wanted to (16:6) – because the Spirit was driving them into Europe. And when Paul would no doubt have liked to found a large Church in Athens (which was still the best known intellectual centre in Europe) still the Holy Spirit frustrated his wishes. For Paul left Athens for Corinth with a sense of failure. He had secured only a few converts in Athens – so few that when writing his first letter to the Corinthians he seems to have forgotten that he had converted anyone at all in 'Greece' (the Roman province of Achaea) before 'Stephanas and his family' in Corinth (1:16, 16:15). His clever appeal to the Athenian intellectuals had not produced the hoped-for results. As he recalled when writing to the Corinthians: 'When I came to you, my brothers . . . I did not use long words and great learning. For I made up my mind to forget everything while I was with you except Jesus Christ, and especially his death on the cross. So when I came to you I was weak and trembled all over with fear, and my teaching and message were not delivered with skilful words of human wisdom, but with convincing proof of the power of God's Spirit.' (2:1-4)

This spiritual power, which built up the Church amid the markets and brothels of Corinth, was so obviously the chief treasure and weapon of the Christians that in *Acts* Simon the magician tried to buy it from Peter (8:18-24) – and Paul the missionary believed that the key question was 'Did you receive the Holy Spirit when you believed?' (19:2) The Spirit was always given, never bought or forced – but always received, never merely hoped for. This in itself makes the Christian message in *Acts* a profound challenge to anyone who regards material possessions or large numbers or elaborate theologies or rich traditions or fine buildings or social status or political relevance as the Church's most desirable asset. The first Christian generation rebukes those of us who, if we were honest about our own spiritual poverty, might well say with the group which Paul met in Ephesus: 'We have not even heard that there is a Holy Spirit.' (19:2)

Around the fact of the living Lord Jesus, every other fact could now be arranged. He was the fulfilment of what had been promised by the prophets in the Old Testament – and to claim that involved nothing less than a claim that this fact of Jesus was the centre of the pattern made by the whole of Jewish life. He was also the fulfilment of the best of what had been said by the Greek philosophers and poets – and to claim that meant claiming that his arrival made possible a new vision of the whole of human life. So the first Christians did not announce the news about Jesus in isolation. They always used this news as the clue in an interpretation of all history and all reality. Jesus was seen as the centre of a vision of the universe.

This has been the task of every generation in the story of Christianity, and in a swiftly changing world many generations have had to tackle the task anew. In the Middle Ages in Western Europe, for example, Jesus was interpreted in terms of the feudal system (his death was the satisfaction due to the outraged honour of God the supreme overlord), or in terms of the newly recovered philosophy of Aristotle (through the writings of St Thomas Aquinas and others) – and all this was miles

and years away from Christianity's original setting,
Palestine. In the Middle Ages in Eastern Europe, Jesus
was interpreted in terms of the power familiar to the
Byzantine empire. In the twentieth century, the significance of Jesus has often been worked out in very different
ways. Jesus has been placed against the new background
provided by the scientific idea of evolution, for example
– or against the more disturbed background provided
by the Marxist idea of revolution. But although these ways
of presenting Jesus have been so vastly different, we can
see two stages in each line of argument. In the first stage,
there is an attempt to secure agreement with non-
Christians that reality is not just a meaningless jumble:
life has a pattern and a purpose. Preferably, of course,
Christians try to secure agreement that this meaning
which runs through the whole of existence can be
expressed by saying, 'I believe in one God.' The second
stage is to work things out at a greater depth, using
wherever possible language which non-Christians will
understand.

In *Acts*, the task of the first Christian generation is
described partly in terms of the appeal to Greeks to
agree on belief in one God, and partly in terms of the
appeal to the Jews to agree that Jesus is the awaited King
of the Jews, the *Messiah*. So we may very quickly take
in turn these beliefs that God is Creator and that Jesus is
Lord.

In Lystra, Barnabas and Paul cite the goodness of nature
as 'proof' of the existence of God. 'The living God, who
made heaven, earth, sea, and all that is in them . . . has
always given proof of himself by the good things he does
. . . he gives you food and fills your hearts with happiness.'
(14:15-17) This is the essence of what has often been
called 'natural religion'.

In Athens, Paul quotes Greek poetry. 'As someone has
said,
  "In him we live and move and exist".'
That 'someone' seems to have been Epimenides the
Cretan – a poet who later in the New Testament, in the
letter to Titus (1:12), appears to be the source of a much

less grand quotation: 'Cretans are always liars, wicked beasts, and lazy gluttons'!

Paul's speech in *Acts* (17:28) continues: 'It is as some of your poets have said,

"We too are his children".'

That seems to be quoted from two poets, Aratus and Cleanthes. In our own time very few people know the names of Epimenides, Aratus, and Cleanthes – but in Paul's day they were famous, and quoting them was a way of linking Paul's message with what was thought to be the best in contemporary pagan thought. For part of Paul's message was that God was the Source of all life and the Father of all – and this belief was shared by many Greeks with the Jews.

But *Acts* is interested chiefly in the place claimed for Jesus within the world of Jewish thought. Apart from his brief reference to 'a man' who was in fact Jesus, Paul's speech in Athens was the kind of thing which we know was being said in the first century by many sympathetic and educated Jews to those Greeks who were prepared to listen. *Acts* shows that it took great courage for Peter, Paul, and their companions to preach to Gentiles, to welcome Gentiles as equals, and to penetrate the Gentile world. But *Acts* also shows that preaching Jesus to the Jews involved nothing less than a religious revolution.

It is understandable that the author of *Acts* was more interested in what Christians said to the Jews – for the Jews so clearly had the best religion of the day, apart from the Christian Way itself. As Paul wrote to the Christians in Rome (9:4-5) about his fellow-Jews: 'They are God's chosen people; he made them his sons and shared his glory with them; he made his covenants with them and gave them the Law; they have the true worship; they have received God's promises; they are descended from the patriarchs, and Christ, as a human being, belongs to their race.' And one reason for the superiority of the Jewish religion over the simple kind of 'natural' religion to which the sermon at Lystra appeals is this: the God of the Jews is a God worshipped through many bitter tragedies. The Old Testament is a library which shows how the Jews struggled to come to terms with the complications and mysteries of life. It includes the *Book of Job*, the most eloquent statement ever written of the problem of evil. The Jews who cling to their worship of God, and to God's promises, are people who know that real life contains more than 'rain from heaven and crops at the right times'.

Naturally the Old Testament was used in the attempt to show that Jesus was properly at the centre of the Jewish world of thought. Here was a library of books which every Jew could be expected to know and to regard as authoritative. It was also the *only* literature which had this status. It was, however, a large library of books, and it seems certain that the Christians soon found it convenient to draw up a list of key quotations from it. This list consisted of passages which had been found effective – or which they hoped would be effective – in settling arguments about Jesus. No such list has survived, but almost all modern scholars believe such lists did exist, and they refer to them as collections of Old Testament 'testimonies'. What Luke seems to have done when writing *Acts* is this. He wrote sermons appropriate to Peter, Stephen, or Paul – and into these sermons he inserted Old Testament quotations as suggested by lists which he possessed. A good many of the same quotations are used elsewhere in the New Testament.

This style of argument often seems remote from the twentieth century. It seems to try to prove a point by quoting a passage which in its original meaning probably meant something quite different. But it is only fair to acknowledge the fact that this way of carrying on a discussion was entirely normal in the first century. Educated Greeks, for example, used the poetry of Homer in this way. Among Jews, the 'rabbis' or teachers were the men who were expert in taking one bit of the Old Testament, comparing it with other bits, and trying to show what it really meant. That was, indeed, how the Jewish tradition was adapted to fresh circumstances. Both Jesus and Paul are known to have been 'rabbis' who taught in this style, for example when they preached in a synagogue. The first chapter of *Acts* represents Peter as quoting psalms from the Old Testament in order to urge the appointment of a new apostle – just as the last chapter of Luke's gospel represents Jesus as quoting passages from 'all the Scriptures, beginning with the books of Moses and the writings of all the prophets' (24:27).

One of the great quotations used in *Acts* is from the Song of the Suffering Servant in chapter 53 of the Book of Isaiah. The Ethiopian official reads the moving words:

> He was like a sheep that is taken to be slaughtered . . .
> He was humiliated, and justice was denied him.

And he asks Philip: 'Tell me, of whom is the prophet saying this? Of himself or of someone else?' This gives Philip the opening he needed. 'Starting from this very passage of scripture, he told him the Good News about Jesus.' (8:35) Here, we can see the permanent meaning easily. Jesus was among the innocent victims of injustice; among the humble, the oppressed, the poor, and the obscure. All three words, so loaded with modern tragedy, can be applied to Jesus: Jewish, Asian, coloured. Jesus took many of the blows of life. He entered the darkness. The news about him is more than news about rain, crops, food, and happiness. It is news about a crucifixion – one of the most horrible deaths ever devised by the cruelty of man.

But it is 'Good News'! Peter's first sermon quotes Psalm 16 about confidence, gladness, and life – about deliverance from death by God. This psalm was then thought to have been written by King David. David had died, so the psalm must refer to someone else – the true *Messiah*, Jesus! As an argument, it sounds weak. As a conviction that God does rescue the humble, the oppressed, the poor, and the obscure, it reflects experience. And Peter goes on to quote Psalm 132:11 about the promise by 'the Lord' that the King's enemies will be brought to the ground, 'as a footstool under your feet'. As a quotation, it does not now seem relevant. But as an expression of the faith that evil will in the end be defeated, it is invincible.

Peter's second sermon, in chapter 3, uses other quotations from the Old Testament. According to *Genesis*, God promised Abraham: 'Through your descendants I will

bless all the people on earth.' That promise had not so
far come true; for the faith of the Jews, the descendants
of Abraham, that they would influence all the nations had
been frustrated by the littleness and the disasters of their
actual history. But through Jesus the Jew, God was
blessing all people on earth! The quotation used was not
an exact quotation, but was a combination of *Deuter-
onomy* 18:15 with *Leviticus* 23:29. It was a promise by
Moses: 'The Lord your God will send you a prophet, just
as he sent me . . . You must listen to everything that he
tells you. Anyone who does not listen to what that
prophet says will be separated from God's people and
destroyed.' There are two Christian ideas here. The first
is that Jesus is the only worthy successor to Moses as the
great leader of God's cause. The second is that to
receive God's blessing through Jesus must mean listening
– and listening must mean turning, or repentance.

Peter's fourth and fifth sermons include further
references to the Old Testament. One of the psalms
(118:22) mentions a stone which the men building the
temple at first thought was useless, yet it turned out to
be the most important stone. The psalm uses that stone
as a symbol of the destiny of the Jewish people – despised,
but useful. Peter sees here a little picture of the supreme
importance of the crucified Jesus (4:11). All the prophets
look forward to a day when God's plans will triumph,
when a new power will bring a new freedom to men. Peter
sees here the longing of many centuries, answered in the
power of Jesus (10:43).

Paul's sermon in chapter 13 picks up some of the more
sombre passages in the prophetic books of the Old
Testament. The prophets, he says, foresaw that their
promises could not be accepted – and how right they
were, although these books are read in every synagogue
'every Sabbath day'! But Paul also quotes from the
psalms some of the most confident promises – promises
that were probably made to Jewish kings at their
coronations. God would be the Father of the King,
giving him the 'sacred and sure blessings' promised to the
first of the kings, David. And Paul argues that these
promises have come true because of God's blessings on

Jesus and the Christians. So this sermon in *Acts* gives the
message which Paul wrote down for the Christians in
Rome (1:2-3). 'The Good News was promised long
ago by God through his prophets, and written in the
Holy Scriptures. It is about his Son, our Lord Jesus
Christ: as to his humanity, he was born descendant of
David . . .'

The word 'Christ' in such a passage is probably treated
by nearly all modern readers as if it were a surname like
'Smith'. Indeed, that is probably how most non-Jewish
hearers or readers reacted when the name 'Jesus Christ'
was put before them in the first century. But of course
there is more to it than that. Since the Greek word
Christos is the equivalent of the Hebrew *Messiah*, meaning the Anointed King promised by the prophets and
eagerly expected by the people, the very phrase 'Jesus
Christ' is like a parcel with a bomb in it. For to admit
that Jesus, who was last seen by the public being tortured
to death as a condemned criminal, really was the
Anointed King to whom all the promises referred –
that was explosive.

A crucified *Messiah*! A Liberator who had suffered
rejection and humiliation! A President who had proved as
vulnerable as a clown! A Superstar who had been
deserted! We cannot be surprised that when in Luke's
gospel there is time for one last sermon from Jesus himself, the sermon is on this theme: 'Was it not necessary
for the *Messiah* to suffer these things and enter his glory?'
(24:26) And we cannot wonder that Peter and Paul in
Acts make the possibility of a suffering *Messiah* –
crucified, yet crowned – the great theme of their attempts
to rearrange the Old Testament around the fact of Jesus
Christ. If the good news about Jesus was to be told to
Jews, it was important to show that 'God long ago
announced by means of all the prophets that his *Messiah*
had to suffer' (3:18). For this would be the great problem
to Jews in Corinth (for example) when they heard Paul
'testifying . . . that Jesus is the *Messiah*' (18:5) – and
later Apollos holding public debates in order to prove
'from the Scriptures that Jesus is the *Messiah*' (18:28).
As Paul acknowledged in his first letter to the Corinthians
(1:23), 'Christ on the cross' made 'a message that is

offensive to the Jews' as well as being 'nonsense to the Gentiles'.

If Christians such as Apollos really did think that they could 'prove' their revolutionary claims about Jesus from the Old Testament, they were wrong (just as Christians were wrong if they thought that they would 'prove' the existence of God from the goodness of nature). It is obviously impossible to demonstrate that the life of Jesus is the only conceivable outcome of the Old Testament's promises and warnings (just as it is impossible to prove that belief in God is the only possible answer to the riddle of the universe). But what must have happened was more modest. Jews who were attracted by Jesus could be helped to overcome what seemed at first the utter scandal of his crucifixion: they could be helped by being shown that his life, with all its tragedy, summed up the Old Testament's spiritually greatest themes. In the very darkness, the light of God was shining.

That task which Peter, Paul, Apollos, and many others discharged in many synagogues and homes in the first century was, as we have seen, done in terms familiar to that century. But it is still relevant, and the same task needs to be done over and over again. The passages which they quoted inevitably mean less to modern readers who are not used to this style of argument – and who are not familiar with the Old Testament. But the themes which emerge are clear to anyone who takes a little trouble to study *Acts*. And they are still the master-themes of the music made by all history – when Jesus is believed. This is what Christian theology, evangelism, or conversation is about.

After the instinctive beliefs of most people that basically life is good, and that all life has a divine Source, there is a further topic: what the divine Fatherhood of all must mean. There is the theme of the Father's compassion on those who are victims of what has gone wrong in the world. There is the theme that God uses the goodness of these people to show what is best and most important. There is the theme that the goodness of those who seem weak is in the end shown to be stronger than anything else in the world. There is the promise that this goodness will win through, however hard this may be to believe. There is the theme that in the end the good man will be shown by God himself to be the real prince among men. When that day comes, God's own Kingship and Fatherhood – his rule and love – will be shown clearly at last.

These are the themes of the whole history of man, according to the vision which has its centre in Jesus. These are themes which need to be stated and restated, generation after generation. If they are themes which find echoes in the heart of any hearer, then that person is not far from sharing the Christian faith. Many heard those themes in the first century, as Christianity won its converts – despite all the slowness and the difficulty. And surely, these are themes which still do get a hearing, even during the twentieth century's rejection of conventional religion.

4. THE FELLOWSHIP OF
     THE SPIRIT

Almost everyone agrees that we need groups in religion
– as in most other human activities. And nowadays
almost everyone is against over-organized religious
institutions. But how can twentieth-century Christians
develop a group life which is not formal or rigid or
constricting? It is a question asked by increasing numbers in our time – for in our time many ask if the Church
can be reborn as 'the fellowship of the Holy Spirit' (Paul's
great phrase at the end of his second letter to the
Corinthians).

Acts contains some clues. It does not provide a blue-
print which we should copy slavishly. But we can find in it
some vital clues, and they are clues about people.

Many of the most effective members of that first
Christian generation are unknown to us by name. We are
not told who founded the Church in Rome, for example.
But we know that it was a strong community when Paul
sent his famous letter preparing for his own first visit to
it – and we know, too, that in that letter he mentions no
apostle or other great figure as being the leader of
Roman Christianity. At the beginning of chapter 9 of
Acts, we are told that Saul of Tarsus was determined to
stamp out 'the Way of the Lord' among the Jews in
Damascus – nearly two hundred miles from Jerusalem.
But how had Christianity got there? We are not told.

Nor are we told who made the vital breakthrough by
first preaching Christianity to non-Jews. Here is all the
evidence that exists: 'some of the believers, men from
Cyprus and Cyrene, went to Antioch and proclaimed the
message to Gentiles also.' (11:20) The names of those
pioneers are for ever lost, one reason being that the author
of *Acts* had no intention of compiling biographies of
everyone who mattered. For example, Titus, who is
prominent in Paul's letters, is never mentioned in *Acts*.

And some of those who *are* mentioned are to us no
more than names. Was the Erastus mentioned once as
one of Paul's helpers (19:22) the same 'Erastus, the city

treasurer', who elsewhere sends greetings to his fellow-Christians (*Romans* 16:23)? Who was 'Mnason, from Cyprus, who had been a believer from the early days' – and was Paul's host in Jerusalem (21:16)? One sentence about the leaders of the church in Antioch (13:1) makes us ask: who was 'Simeon called the Black'? Was he Simon of Cyrene, who carried the cross of Jesus and became 'the father of Alexander and Rufus' (*Mark* 15:21)? Who were Lucius from Cyrene, and Manaean? The latter, we are told, had been brought up as a boy with Herod the tetrarch – the very man who 'made fun of Jesus' and 'became friends' with Pilate (*Luke* 23:6-12). Another sentence (20:4) makes us ask: who were Sopater, Gaius, Tychicus, Trophimus? Were Aristarchus and Secundus (whose name means Second) twins? We do not have more than their names, yet they were picked as Paul's companions in his very important last journey to Jerusalem, and some of their names recur in letters by him or attributed to him. Little is said in *Acts* about men such as Timothy and Silas, shown by Paul's letters (and Peter's) to have been key figures in the Church.

But some people are portrayed more fully in *Acts* – and these references help us to understand why the message embodied in such personalities proved so attractive.

There is, for example, Ananias. He is 'a religious man who obeyed our Law and was highly respected by all the Jews living in Damascus' (22:12). He has become a Christian (it seems, some time ago) and has been told by many people 'about all the terrible things' done by Saul of Tarsus. Naturally he is highly suspicious of such a notorious persecutor of the Church. He himself sounds like a gentle man, moving easily from the Jewish Law to the Christian discipleship; a popular man, trusted as a friend and told the news by Jews and Christians alike. Such a man would be deeply shocked by Saul's violence. But once he is convinced that this man has been chosen as a servant of God, he is ready to pay the price of his conviction. He goes straight up to him in the house of Judas in Straight Street (the main commercial street in Damascus), and he speaks two words which are epoch-making because they are enough to greet the new member of the Church: *Brother Saul!* (9:17)

It was Ananias who baptized Saul. But it was Barnabas who brought him into the inner circle of the Church.

Barnabas is presented to us as 'One who Encourages' (4:36) – although why it was ever believed that the Greek name Barnabas actually means that is a mystery. He is a Levite; he belongs to a family with the hereditary right to assist the priests in the Jerusalem temple. In his case, this has become an honorary connection with the cathedral (so to speak), for he is a landowner in Cyprus. When he becomes a Christian he sells 'a field', we are told; presumably this is a modest reference to the disposal of a sizeable agricultural property. He 'brought the money and turned it over to the apostles'. That must have been a financial encouragement to the Church, to begin with.

More is to come in the account which *Acts* gives of Barnabas. For it is he who encourages the apostles to welcome the man who is to become the greatest of them all. 'Saul went to Jerusalem and tried to join the disciples. They would not believe, however, that he was a disciple, and they were all afraid of him. Then Barnabas came to his help and took him to the apostles.' (9:26-7) But Paul's letter to the Galatians (if it refers to the same incident) shows that this is not the whole truth about a very tense situation. The polite account in *Acts* implies some humility in Saul of Tarsus, but the letter recalls his real mood, one of great touchiness. 'I did not go to anyone for advice,' he boasts. 'It was three years later that I went to Jerusalem to get information from Peter, and I stayed with him for two weeks. I did not see any other apostle except James, the Lord's brother. What I write is true, I am not lying, so help me God!' (1:16-20) This letter shows how near to impossible must have been the work of reconciling Saul to the leaders of the Church: for Saul implies that he was seeking *information*, not fellowship, and that he was too busy to see more than a couple of the apostles! Yet this work of reconciliation is a job which Barnabas undertakes on his own initiative.

Later in *Acts*, it is the reconciling Barnabas who is chosen to make the contacts between the Jerusalem church and the first Gentile Christians in Antioch. He executes this mission perfectly. 'He was glad and urged them all to be faithful and true to the Lord with all their hearts. Barnabas was a good man, full of the Holy Spirit and faith.' (11:23-4) But he does not rest content with establishing harmony. He risks upsets by going 'to Tarsus to look for Saul' (11:25) – a phrase which implies that at this stage Saul is making himself invisible in his home town. It is Barnabas who summons Saul to become a leader of the Church in Antioch.

When that community decides to send out its own missionaries, it chooses 'Barnabas and Saul' (13:2). The seniority of Barnabas is emphasized by the fact that the missionaries go first to Cyprus, his home country. But once in Cyprus, Barnabas acknowledges his junior's greater gifts, so that when the team leaves the island it is as 'Paul and his companions' (13:13). But even after this, when in Lystra pagans begin to worship them in belief that 'the gods have become like men and have come down to us', it is Barnabas who is worshipped as Zeus the majestic father of the gods, talkative little Paul being classified only as the gods' messenger, Hermes (14:11-12). It is the true greatness of Barnabas that he does not behave like Zeus, although he looks like him.

And the rare quality of his personal relations is to be tested again. He was the champion of Saul of Tarsus when Saul was alone and truculent, the underdog; now he supports John Mark, an unreliable young man who is disapproved of by Paul the established missionary. When Barnabas and Saul went to Cyprus, 'they had John Mark with them to help in the work' (13:5). But when they moved on from Cyprus back to Asia Minor, 'John Mark left them there and went back to Jerusalem' (13:13). Later, when Paul wished to undertake a second great journey from Antioch, John Mark was back on the scene and 'Barnabas wanted to take John Mark with them' (15:37). When Paul indignantly refuses to allow this, Barnabas takes the young man's side. 'They had a sharp argument between them, and separated from each other. Barnabas took Mark and sailed off for Cyprus . . .' (15:39) Thus he disappears from *Acts*. But he does not disappear from our affection; for we feel now that Barnabas has defended John Mark because the young man needs encouragement and not only because (as is stated in the letter to the Colossians, 4:10) John Mark is his sister's son.

The character of John Mark is best discussed when commenting on Mark's gospel, not on these *Acts*. Here we can only note that Paul's letters show that he was reconciled to the young man, who became his assistant again – and that tradition makes Mark also the assistant of Peter and the founder of the church of Alexandria. The first letter of Peter (5:13) refers to 'my son Mark'.

Let us turn instead to a girl who must have been well known to John Mark. She seems to have been about the same age, and she is mentioned in *Acts* because she works in the house of his mother, Mary, in Jerusalem. Her name is Rhoda, or Rose.

She is only a servant, perhaps only a slave. She has probably heard little of the conversation in the house, and understood less, although the house has become the Christian headquarters. It is reasonable to suppose that in the large upper room of this house Jesus held his last supper (which Rhoda laid and cleared up) and that the Holy Spirit was first experienced in the same room, with Rhoda in the background. But Rhoda has understood enough to react in a very characteristic way when Peter knocks at the outside door on his escape from prison. 'She recognized Peter's voice and was so happy that she ran back in without opening the door.' (12:14) Peter has become her friend, but she keeps him waiting because she has lost her wits. She wants to pass the news immediately to the others, who are also her friends – although they at once tell her: 'You are crazy!'

The simplicity of Rhoda's affection was, we say, natural. And surely, it is not *only* Christians who show love and courage! Paul's own relations may or may not have been Christians; the question is not answered when we are told that 'the son of Paul's sister' bravely entered a Roman fort in order to inform both the imprisoned Paul and the Roman commander about a plot (23:12-22). That may have been just a young man's loyal courage. But in the first of his surviving letters, Paul tells us plainly that virtues which anyone can recognize and find attractive are to him the most important harvest of the Holy Spirit in the lives of Christians. 'The Spirit produces love, joy, peace, patience, kindness, goodness, faithfulness, humility, and self-control.' (*Galatians* 5:22) And it is clear that courage and these other characteristics, which all could recognize, were the early Christians' chief weapons in converting others. In the long run, we may guess, what Rhoda did simply by being herself proved more influential than any eloquence possessed by Philip's 'four unmarried daughters who proclaimed God's message' (21:9) – for it was by goodness that Christian slaves impressed their owners, Christian wives their husbands, Christian nobodies their friends.

Inevitably we catch only rare glimpses of this person-to-person influence at work in *Acts*. But one glimpse is fascinating, for it is a glimpse of a community which included 'many of the leading women' (17:4) – and was not shocked when they went on leading.

At the beginning of chapter 18, we are introduced in Corinth to 'a Jew named Aquila, born in Pontus, who had just come from Italy with his wife Priscilla, because Emperor Claudius had ordered all the Jews to leave Rome. Paul went to see them, and stayed and worked with them, because he earned his living by making tents, just as they did.' Were Aquila and Priscilla already Christians, or did their lodger (and employee?) convert them? We are not told. In the middle of the chapter, however, we are told that 'Priscilla and Aquila' accompanied Paul to Ephesus. In the ancient world, it was most unusual to put the wife's name first. As is notorious, passages in Paul's own letters preach the subjection of women. But in this Christian marriage nineteen hundred years ago Priscilla was liberated. And by the end of the chapter, we find that the couple have another theologian as a lodger: 'A certain Jew named Apollos, born in Alexandria, . . . an eloquent speaker' who 'had a thorough knowledge of the Scriptures' and who 'with great enthusiasm spoke and taught correctly the facts about Jesus.' It was not enough to know the facts about Jesus: a Christian must also share the Holy Spirit. So this couple give something more than hospitality to the clever and eloquent Apollos. 'When Priscilla and Aquila heard him, they took him home with them and explained to him more correctly the Way of God.' (18:26) This Apollos had such intellectual and spiritual gifts to offer the Church that later on Paul had to send his first letter to the Corinthians to warn some who were trying to set up a faction with the slogan. 'I am with Apollos.' (1:12) And many have suggested that Apollos wrote the *Letter to the Hebrews* now in the New Testament.

This 'Way of God' must have been shown correctly in the life of many first-century Christian homes. To some of us, the very idea is embarrassing because it suggests sentimentality, hypocrisy, paternalism and wife-slavery. But the Christian home need not be as frightful as that. It can be a place of outgoing hospitality and radiating happiness. Certainly there is a whole church which gathers around Aquila and Priscilla and 'meets in their house', as Paul's first letter to the Corinthians shows (16:19). And the Christian family can breed in all its members a strength of character which we can only admire. Certainly in Paul's letter to the Christians in Rome there are greetings 'to Priscilla and Aquila, my fellow workers in the service of Christ Jesus, who risked their lives for me. I am grateful to them – not only I, but all the Gentile churches as well.' (16:3, 4)

In *Acts* many families join the Church through baptism *as families*. Examples provided by *Acts* are the family of Cornelius (11:14), Lydia 'and the people of her house' (16:15), the jailer in Philippi 'and all his family' (16:33), Crispus the leader of the synagogue in Corinth 'and all his family' (18:8). In some cases, presumably these households included children – and also wives and servants who were not as soundly converted as the master of the household. The religion of *Acts* is, wherever possible, a family affair.

As was only natural in the ancient world, the New Testament usually expected a woman's place to be in the home. But *Acts* also shows us that women away from their families had a place in early Christianity. Already in the first chapter we meet the 'women' meeting with the apostles (1:14). Presumably these were 'the women who had followed Jesus from Galilee' (*Luke* 23:55). From an early date it has been suggested that these included the apostles' wives. In his first letter to the Corinthians (9:5)

Paul asked: 'Don't I have the right to do what the other apostles do, and the Lord's brothers, and Peter, and take a Christian wife with me on my journeys?' But there can be no doubt that this group also included women without husbands, such as Martha and Mary who appear in the gospels – or the widows who appear in *Acts* (6:1). Jerusalem contained an unusual number of widows because some devout Jews made a practice of spending their last days in the Holy City and being buried there.

In his gospel Luke often pays special attention to women. There is the same interest in *Acts* – for example, in the story of Tabitha and the 'shirts and coats' she made (9:36-43). But in general, the women of the first Christian generation were held in such honour by the men that Paul (who is often falsely accused of anti-feminism) could remind the Galatians: 'there is no difference between Jews and Gentiles, between slaves and free men, between men and women; you are all one in union with Christ Jesus.' (3:28)

When Paul was approaching Rome as a prisoner, some Christians went out from the city to the two villages known as the Market of Appius and Three Inns, in order to greet him. 'When Paul saw them, he thanked God and took courage.' (28:15) That may well be our response to this whole account of the men and women of the first Christian generation. But what held these Christians together, 'in union with Christ Jesus'? One answer to this question is very simple and very important. They were all baptized.

Peter is asked by 'the people' on the first Whitsunday: 'What shall we do, brother?' And he answers: 'Turn away from your sins, each one of you, and be baptized in the name of Jesus Christ, so that your sins will be forgiven; and you will receive God's gift, the Holy Spirit.' (2:37-8) Whether or not this reproduces Peter's exact words, it clearly shows the supreme importance of baptism among the first Christians. This was definitely part of 'the Good News about Jesus', not an optional extra. When Philip told 'the Good News' to the Ethiopian, it must have included baptism, for the official asked there and then: 'Here is some water. What is to keep me from being baptized?' (8:36) When Paul 'preached the word of the Lord' to the jailer in prison at Philippi, the jailer and his family were 'baptized at once' (16:33).

Baptism was profoundly symbolic. It meant becoming a Christian or being identified with 'the name of Jesus Christ'. This was dramatized by immersing the candidate in a river wherever possible – not only because John the Baptist had used the river Jordan, but also because going under the water felt for a moment like a little death and baptism was identification with Jesus Christ who had been crucified. As the new Christian emerged from the water, he or she could look forward to a new life and to the gift of the Holy Spirit. It was like a second birth.

We do not know as much as we should like. There was no river in that prison in Philippi, and we do not know how water was poured over the jailer and his family. That night it was all over in a matter of hours – but we do not know what preparation was normally given to candidates. We are told that the jailer's family were baptized, but we are not told whether this included children too young to understand or adults too sceptical to be converted fully there and then.

We do not know what was the relationship between Christian baptism and 'the baptism of John'. Was Apollos, who arrived in Ephesus knowing 'only the baptism of John' (18:25), now given a Christian baptism which he had previously lacked? Were all the apostles baptized, and if so by whom? We do not even know when the Trinitarian phrase quoted at the end of Matthew's gospel ('Baptize them in the name of the Father, the Son, and the Holy Spirit', 28:19) became standard. And baptism's connection with the gift of the Holy Spirit was not routine. Sometimes there was a delay which may well have been puzzling. For example, we read that when Christianity first spread to Samaria 'the Holy Spirit had not yet come down on any of them; they had only been baptized in the name of the Lord Jesus' (8:16). Sometimes the Holy Spirit was given *before* baptism, as it was to 'all those who were listening' to Peter's sermon in Caesarea (10:44-8).

But there can be no doubt of the general importance of baptism in the Church described by *Acts*. There can also be no doubt that baptism was regarded as only the beginning of 'the Way' for an individual. Each convert who had been baptized was expected to learn and grow by joining himself or herself to the Christian community's life. And although that life changed greatly across the years, and across the miles from Jerusalem to Rome and beyond, it never in spirit moved far from the brotherhood of the baptized in the first weeks, when 'they spent their time in learning from the apostles, taking part in the fellowship, and sharing in the fellowship meals and the prayers' (2:42).

The apostles' teaching is obviously vital – and we know that a reverence for the apostles was widespread in the first Christian century. One piece of evidence is the reference to 'the twelve apostles' as foundation stones in *The Revelation to John* (21:14). But we have already noticed how little *Acts* tells us about the original twelve. They are not mentioned after 16:4. This is distinctly odd, when we are told at the beginning how much care was taken to replace Judas Iscariot by Matthias (1:21-6).

On the other hand, *Acts* does give us two or three clues. The first is the number twelve – the number of the tribes of Israel. By making their number up to twelve after the tragedy of Judas Iscariot, the apostles showed themselves to be well aware that the followers of Jesus were meant to be the new Israel, the new People of God, – and that the twelve apostles were meant to symbolize this. But when James, the brother of John, was 'put to death by the sword' (12:2), the martyrdom of that apostle was *not* followed by the choice of another to fill the vacancy. It seems that the point made by the original number twelve did not need to be repeated endlessly, once it had been made clear that the fellowship of the followers of Jesus was not to consist of a casual meeting of individuals at their own convenience.

Another clue to the role of the apostles is provided by Peter's account of the qualifications needed before the choice of Matthias. 'He must be one of those who were in our group during the whole time that the Lord Jesus travelled about with us, beginning from the time John preached his baptism until the day Jesus was taken up from us to heaven.' (1:22) In other words, the apostles must be people who can give the history of Jesus because they were eye-witnesses. This teaching could no longer be given by word of mouth when first James and then the others of the twelve were silenced by death or other causes. It was presumably to meet the need of a more permanent record after about the year 65 that, as Luke tells us at the beginning of his gospel: 'Many have done their best to write a report of the things that have taken place among us. They wrote what we have been told by those who saw these things from the beginning and proclaimed the message.'

The third clue comes when *Acts* tells of the appointment of seven helpers 'in order to handle finances'. The apostles then limit their own job: 'We ... will give our full time to prayers and the work of preaching.' (6:4) It is clear that, although Peter had handled the crisis created by the dishonesty of Ananias and Sapphira, the apostles did not regard themselves as managers in any general sense – for no wise manager leaves all financial matters and all the practical decisions to others! Gradually the practical importance of the apostles in church life in Jerusalem must have diminished, although no doubt their prayers and sermons were invaluable. We can tell this from chapter 11. In the first sentence, 'the apostles and the brothers throughout all of Judea' are mentioned because they 'heard that the Gentiles also had received the word of God' – but when the new Christians in Antioch decide to send money 'to help their brothers who lived in Judea', there is silence about the apostles. 'They ... sent the money to the church elders.' (11:30)

Is the explanation of the disappearance of the apostles from *Acts* that they left Jerusalem? We simply do not know. For some time, they must have thought it their duty to stick together in Jerusalem. We are told that during the 'cruel persecution' which included the stoning of Stephen, 'all the believers, *except the apostles*, were scattered' (8:1). But later on, the apostles may well have acted in the spirit of the words of Jesus in *Acts*: 'you will be witnesses for me ... to the ends of the earth.' (1:8)

What appears from *Acts* is that Philip was the first leader to take the gospel to Samaria in the north (8:5) – and to a traveller on 'the road that goes from Jerusalem to Gaza' in the south (8:26). But this Philip was 'the evangelist' and 'one of the seven men who had been chosen in Jerusalem'; he was not the apostle Philip (21:8). Among the apostles, Peter was, without question, the spokesman on the first Whitsunday. In the next chapters Peter and John are prominent, and they are the apostles sent to Samaria after the missionary work of Philip and others (8:14-25). This experience – which included preaching the 'Good News in many villages in Samaria' on the way back to Jerusalem – seems to have encouraged Peter greatly, for before long we read that 'Peter travelled everywhere' (9:32).

This is the earliest record we have of an apostle becoming a mobile evangelist like Philip. And it is an impressive record, for it suggests that Peter sacrificed the prestige and comparative security of the leadership of the church in Jerusalem in order to spread 'the Good News' – just as Philip had chosen an evangelist's life in exchange for the ordered routine of issuing with the other seven 'helpers' in Jerusalem a pension to Greek-speaking widows.

It is clear that Simon Peter retained a great moral authority in the Christian fellowship. How could it be otherwise? As Luke's gospel reminds us (5:10) this fisherman had been the first disciple to be called by Jesus, and had been promised, 'from now on you will be catching men.' The same gospel names Simon first among the apostles (6:14), and quotes Simon the Rock's momentous insight: 'You are God's *Messiah*!' (9:20) Finally the gospel gives us the Easter picture of Peter running before any other man to the empty tomb of Jesus (24:12), and being rewarded by an appearance of the risen Lord: 'The Lord is risen indeed! He has appeared to Simon!' (24:34) Such a man as Simon the Rock could never be treated as merely one among many leaders of the Church. It is no surprise to read that 'after a long debate Peter stood up' – and by his speech obtained a respectful silence in 'the whole group' for the report by Barnabas and Paul (15:7, 12)

But astonishingly enough, that is Peter's last appearance in *Acts*. Peter's last recorded speech harks back to the time in Joppa when Captain Cornelius was baptized, and the Holy Spirit was given to him and other Gentiles. 'A long time ago God chose me from among you to preach the Good News to the Gentiles.' (15:7) But *Acts* makes clear that history robbed Peter of the proud title of Apostle to the Gentiles. Paul makes it even clearer in his letter to the Galatians: 'by God's power I was made an apostle to the Gentiles, just as Peter was made an apostle to the Jews.' (2:8)

There is no reason to doubt the tradition of the Church from a very early date that in death Peter and Paul were not divided. There is also no reason why the early traditions should not be true that Paul was released from Rome and had a further period as a mobile evangelist (in Spain and elsewhere) before his final arrest and execution, while Peter settled in Rome as the first great leader of the church there before his own martyrdom. We know from Paul's letters that Peter and his wife made many journeys, and that his fame and influence were widespread. For example, one of the factions forming in the church in Corinth had the slogan, 'I am with Peter.' However, these things are not in *Acts*.

What *Acts* does give us is a glimpse of the extraordinary career of James the brother of Jesus.

We know from Paul's first letter to the Corinthians that according to tradition the risen Christ 'appeared to James' (15:7), and from Paul's letter to the Galatians that James came to be mentioned before Peter among the Christian leaders in Jerusalem: 'James, Peter, and John, who seemed to be the leaders . . .' (2:9) Yet James was apparently not considered as a possible member of the twelve when Matthias was chosen, and the explanation seems to be that he had not been with Jesus since the Nazareth years. While Jesus was teaching and healing, Jesus's mother and brothers did not support him, so that Jesus once declared: 'My mother and brothers are those who hear the word of God and obey it.' (*Luke* 8:21) Luke's gospel does not name Mary among 'the women who had followed (Jesus) from Galilee' to the cross and the grave (23:49, 55), but *Acts* includes 'Mary the mother of Jesus, and his brothers' among the disciples who 'gathered frequently to pray as a group' immediately after the end of the resurrection appearances (1:14). It has often been pointed out that these appearances were not made to sceptics. But Jesus's brother James may have been converted as Saul of Tarsus was by an Easter event.

It is not surprising that the relatives of Jesus received special honour among their fellow-Christians. History tells us of a number of religious leaders whose families carried on their leadership after their deaths. But in the case of early Christianity, the Founder's kin were not given 'royal family' treatment. Hegesippus, a Christian who wrote in about 180 (and is quoted extensively in the *Ecclesiastical History* of Eusebius), tells a curious story. About ninety years previously the grandchildren of Jude, another of Jesus's brothers, had been interrogated. The Romans had suspected them of possible treason, as being descended from King David and as being related to the troublesome 'Christ'. But the Romans had decided that they were harmless. They had said that their only ambitions were heavenly – and had shown their hardened workmen's hands to prove it.

James seems to have become the leader of the church in Jerusalem on merit. At any rate, by chapter 15 of *Acts* he has so built up his position among the Christians in Jerusalem that he gives his opinion to end the crucial debate of the 'apostles and the elders' about the terms on which Gentiles are to be admitted to the Church. Before very long the apostles have vanished and this is what we read: 'Paul went with us to see James; and all the church elders were present.' (21:18)

Such a rise argues that James was, so to speak, a statesman in the Church. But Hegesippus gives a picture of a man who was far more than a chairman. 'He received the name of "the Just" from all men, from the time of the Lord even to our own; for there were many called James ... He anointed himself not with oil, and used no bath ... And alone he entered the sanctuary, and was found on his knees asking forgiveness on behalf of the people, so that his knees became hard like a camel's . . .' The same account records that he was stoned and clubbed to death by Jews in Jerusalem, some years before the city fell to the Romans.

In the first century, the Church had strong leadership. But to lead the Christian Church meant having knees like a camel and dying like a rat.

We are given, therefore, a picture of church leadership which has two striking features: it was flexible, and it was holy. It is clear that what kept the brotherhood of the baptized together was not a legal or administrative dominance by 'the apostles' in Jerusalem.

Indeed, *Acts* once quietly calls Paul and Barnabas 'apostles' (14:3) – thus breaking any monopoly claimed by, or on behalf of, the original twelve. This quiet sentence about Paul and Barnabas ('the apostles stayed there for a long time') is in contrast with the passionate affirmations in Paul's own letters about his own apostleship – but is perhaps equally effective. To justify his right to be called an 'apostle', Paul could point to his experience of the risen Lord on the Damascus road, but so far as we know Barnabas had been neither the companion of Jesus nor the recipient of a 'resurrection' appearance. The implication seems to be radical: what makes an apostle is spreading the 'Good News' with a special call and a special courage. Such a radical attitude explains why in his letter to the Romans Paul refers to Andronicus and Junias, who 'became Christians before I did', as 'well known among the apostles' (16:7). Barnabas, Paul, Andronicus, Junias, and perhaps many more were 'apostles' in this broader sense. In his first letter to the Corinthians (4:9-13), Paul passionately describes their working conditions, so different from those of the honoured twelve in Jerusalem. 'It seems to me that God has given us apostles the very last place, like men condemned to die in public, as a spectacle for the whole world of angels and of men. For Christ's sake we are fools . . . We are weak . . . We are despised . . . We go hungry and thirsty; we are clothed in rags; we are beaten; we wander from place to place . . . We are cursed . . . we are persecuted . . . we are insulted . . . We are no more than this world's garbage; we are the scum of the earth to this very hour!'

We should expect to find that exceptionally strong personalities among the apostles, evangelists, and other leaders did not hesitate to give orders – and to speak or write in an intimately personal way – to the congregations with which they had special relationships. In fact, we have in the New Testament the letters of Paul and John, and we have in *Acts* Paul's magnificent farewell speech to the elders of Ephesus (20:17-38), showing how frankly a father-in-God could deal with Christians who loved him and who accepted his spiritual authority. But in the period covered by *Acts*, there is no evidence that the apostles or anyone else 'governed' the Church in a systematic way.

We should expect each Christian congregation to have 'elders' as leaders – as each Jewish synagogue had. At least we know from *Acts* that its author took this for granted in the churches which Paul and Barnabas founded, for we read: 'In each church they appointed elders for them; and with prayers and fasting they commended them to the Lord, in whom they had put their trust.' (14:23)

From the Greek word for 'elders' (*presbuteroi*), our 'presbyters' (or 'priests', a shorter word) has come. No doubt initially these 'elders' would be appointed by the founders of their churches – by the apostles jointly in Jerusalem, or by evangelists such as Paul. But the New Testament does not solemnly insist on 'elders'. Indeed, in Antioch – the home church of Paul and Barnabas – the leaders seem to be called 'prophets and teachers' (13:1), not 'elders'. We know that wandering 'prophets' were prominent in the Church early in the second century, and within the New Testament we have in the letter to Ephesians a rather significant list: the ascended Christ 'appointed some to be apostles, others to be prophets, others to be evangelists, others to be pastors and teachers' (4:11).

We should also bear in mind two other points about the leadership.

In the first place, *Acts* does not state the threefold division which soon became the rule of the Catholic Church – bishop, priest, deacon. Although deacons appear in the letters to the Philippians and to Timothy, they are not mentioned in *Acts*; the seven 'helpers' in Jerusalem (6:1-6) are not called deacons.

There are not even separate bishops in *Acts*. The elders of Ephesus are called 'overseers' (20:28), and from the Greek word for this (*episkopoi*) our 'bishops' has come. But the rise of the bishops belongs to the period after the close of *Acts* – a period for which other books of the New Testament begin to supply some evidence. In that period, strong local leadership became vital. The apostles and the first evangelists such as Philip and Barnabas were dead or old, and there was danger of confusion in teaching; the Roman empire was beginning its persecutions, and a vigorous, united response under a clearly acknowledged authority had to be made; and in any case, as the Church left behind its initial period of enthusiasm, guidance which was wise, competent, and patient was essential. Within the age of *Acts*, it is enough for Paul to speak as a father-in-God to the elders of Ephesus, about 'the flock which the Holy Spirit has placed in your care' (20:28).

Secondly, there are very few Christians in *Acts* who are paid to be Christians. Paul himself is content to work for considerable periods as a tent-maker. He holds up his hands and says: 'You yourselves know that with these hands of mine I have worked and provided everything that my companions and I have needed.' (20:34) He is not fanatical about earning his living in this way. We gain the impression in the later chapters of *Acts* that he has somehow come into money – that he is able to be generous to fellow-Jews in Jerusalem, to finance himself and some companions during a long imprisonment and a series of trials, to seem the sort of man able to bribe a Roman governor (24:26), and finally to hire a house in Rome (28:30). We know from his letters that Paul saw nothing wrong in principle with the apostles or a few others earning their living by preaching and he himself received financial gifts 'more than once', as he recalls when writing to the Philippians (4:16). But the fact that Paul works as a tent-maker is a useful reminder of the fact that the elders leading the congregations are honorary. In *Acts*, the Church does not depend on paid professionals.

What kept the first Christians together was not organization. It was the conviction that the living Jesus was among them – and able to speak up for himself. We see this in *The Revelation to John*, with its vision of Christ in glory speaking to the seven churches of Asia. The Christians received or strengthened this vision when they were together in fellowship. But, to quote again the pregnant phrase in *Acts*, Christian fellowship then meant nothing formal – just sharing 'the fellowship meals and the prayers' (2:42).

The 'fellowship meals' were real (although not big) suppers, eaten in one of the Christian homes, as Paul's first letter to the Corinthians shows (11:17-34). But they also included those moments, inexhaustible in their meaning, which recalled the Last Supper described by Luke in his gospel (22:14-23). And they were regular. Thus we read in *Acts* about Paul's last visit to Troas: 'On Saturday evening we gathered together for the fellowship meal.' (20:7) That night was chosen because it was the night during which the Lord rose. So Paul 'broke bread, and ate' – and continued 'talking with them for a long time until sunrise' (20:11). As the Christians dispersed in the early light, it no doubt reminded some of them how according to the tradition about the first Easter 'very early on Sunday morning the women went to the grave carrying the spices they had prepared.' (*Luke* 24:1)

The 'prayers' were said at first 'every day' in the temple at Jerusalem, as well as in private homes (2:46). But Christian prayer did not depend on sacred surroundings or domestic security. Thus we read in the story of the prison in Philippi: 'About midnight Paul and Silas were praying and singing hymns to God, and the other prisoners were listening to them.' (16:25) And that is probably the most characteristic glimpse we are ever likely to catch of the brotherhood of the baptized. Around, it was night. And there was a sense of imprisonment, for the first century was felt by many who lived through it to be a dark age, an age of fear – under a ruthless empire, in a corrupt society, with a great deal of mental illness because people were afraid of many things. The Christian Church in particular could have produced many reasons for being imprisoned by fear. But it was a fellowship which held together in the darkness and under unpopularity. As if by instinct it sang to God, because it was created and led by the Holy Spirit, God's tempest. And it was a fellowship where experience frequently vindicated promises such as those made in Paul's letter to the Philippians (written when he was again a prisoner): 'God's peace, which is far beyond human understanding, will keep your hearts and minds safe, in union with Christ Jesus . . . My God, with all his abundant wealth in Christ Jesus, will supply all your needs.' (4:7, 19)

It is not necessary, or possible, to imitate *Acts* in every detail. But the few essentials are plain – and permanent. A twentieth-century fellowship which possesses this peace and wealth will spread its good news by its own acts.

THE ACTS OF THE APOSTLES

1 Dear Theophilus:
In my first book I wrote about all the things that Jesus did and taught, from the time he began his work ²until the day he was taken up to heaven. Before he was taken up he gave instructions by the power of the Holy Spirit to the men he had chosen as his apostles. ³For forty days after his death he showed himself to them many times, in ways that proved beyond doubt that he was alive; he was seen by them, and talked with them about the Kingdom of God. ⁴And when they came together, he gave them this order, "Do not leave Jerusalem, but wait for the gift my Father promised, that I told you about. ⁵John baptized with water, but in a few days you will be baptized with the Holy Spirit."

Jesus Is Taken up to Heaven

⁶When the apostles met together with Jesus they asked him, "Lord, will you at this time give the Kingdom back to Israel?"

⁷Jesus said to them, "The times and occasions are set by my Father's own authority, and it is not for you to know when they will be. ⁸But you will be filled with power when the Holy Spirit comes on you, and you will be witnesses for me in Jerusalem, in all of Judea and Samaria, and to the ends of the earth." ⁹After saying this, he was taken up to heaven as they watched him; and a cloud hid him from their sight.

¹⁰They still had their eyes fixed on the sky as he went away, when two men dressed in white suddenly stood beside them. ¹¹"Men of Galilee," they said, "why do you stand there looking up at the sky? This Jesus, who was taken up from you into heaven, will come back in the same way that you saw him go to heaven."

Judas' Successor

¹²Then the apostles went back to Jerusalem from the Mount of Olives, which is about half a mile away from the city. ¹³They entered Jerusalem and went up to the

room where they were staying: Peter, John, James and
Andrew, Philip and Thomas, Bartholomew and Matthew, James, the son of Alphaeus, Simon the Patriot,
and Judas, the son of James. [14]They gathered frequently
to pray as a group, together with the women, and with
Mary the mother of Jesus, and his brothers.

[15]A few days later there was a meeting of the believers, about one hundred and twenty in all, and Peter
stood up to speak. [16]"My brothers," he said, "the
scripture had to come true in which the Holy Spirit,
speaking through David, predicted about Judas, who
was the guide of those who arrested Jesus. [17]Judas was
a member of our group, because he had been chosen to
have a part in our work."

[18](With the money that Judas got for his evil act he
bought a field, where he fell to his death; he burst open
and all his insides spilled out. [19]All the people living in
Jerusalem heard about it, and so in their own language
they call that field Akeldama, which means "Field of
Blood.")

[20]"For it is written in the book of Psalms,
'May his house become empty;
    let no one live in it.'
It is also written,
'May someone else take his place of
    service.'

[21-22]"So then, someone must join us as a witness to
the resurrection of the Lord Jesus. He must be one of
those who were in our group during the whole time
that the Lord Jesus travelled about with us, beginning
from the time John preached his baptism until the day
Jesus was taken up from us to heaven."

[23]So they proposed two men: Joseph, who was called
Barsabbas (he was also called Justus), and Matthias.
[24]Then they prayed, "Lord, you know the hearts of all
men. And so, Lord, show us which one of these two
you have chosen [25]to take this place of service as an
apostle which Judas left to go to the place where he
belongs." [26]Then they drew lots to choose between the
two names. The name chosen was that of Matthias,
and he was added to the group of the eleven apostles.

The Coming of the Holy Spirit

2 When the day of Pentecost arrived, all the believers were gathered together in one place. ²Suddenly there was a noise from the sky which sounded like a strong wind blowing, and it filled the whole house where they were sitting. ³Then they saw what looked like tongues of fire spreading out; and each person there was touched by a tongue. ⁴They were all filled with the Holy Spirit and began to talk in other languages, as the Spirit enabled them to speak.

⁵There were Jews living in Jerusalem, religious men who had come from every country in the world. ⁶When they heard this noise, a large crowd gathered. They were all excited, because each one of them heard the believers talking in his own language. ⁷In amazement and wonder they exclaimed, "These men who are talking like this— they are all Galileans! ⁸How is it, then, that all of us hear them speaking in our own native language? ⁹We are from Parthia, Media, and Elam; from Mesopotamia, Judea, and Cappadocia; from Pontus and Asia, ¹⁰from Phrygia and Pamphylia, from Egypt and the regions of Libya near Cyrene; some of us are from Rome, ¹¹both Jews and Gentiles converted to Judaism; and some of us are from Crete and Arabia—yet all of us hear them speaking in our own languages of the great things that God has done!" ¹²Amazed and confused they all kept asking each other, "What does this mean?"

¹³But others made fun of the believers, saying, "These men are drunk!"

Peter's Message

¹⁴Then Peter stood up with the other eleven apostles, and in a loud voice began to speak to the crowd, "Fellow Jews, and all of you who live in Jerusalem, listen to me and let me tell you what this means. ¹⁵These men are not drunk, as you suppose; it is only nine o'clock in the morning. ¹⁶Rather, this is what the prophet Joel spoke about,

¹⁷ 'This is what I will do in the last days, God says:

Listen to me

    I will pour out my Spirit upon all men.
  Your sons and your daughters will
      prophesy;
    your young men will see visions,
    and your old men will dream dreams.
18 Yes, even on my slaves, both men and
      women,
    I will pour out my Spirit in those days,
    and they will prophesy.
19 I will perform miracles in the sky above,
    and marvels on the earth below.
  There will be blood, and fire, and thick
      smoke;
20   the sun will become dark,
    and the moon red as blood,
    before the great and glorious Day of the
      Lord arrives.
21 And then, whoever calls on the name of
    the Lord will be saved.'
22 "Listen to these words, men of Israel! Jesus of
Nazareth was a man whose divine mission was clearly
shown to you by the miracles, wonders, and signs which

God did through him; you yourselves know this, for it took place here among you. ²³God, in his own will and knowledge, had already decided that Jesus would be handed over to you; and you killed him, by letting sinful men nail him to the cross. ²⁴But God raised him from the dead; he set him free from the pains of death, because it was impossible that death should hold him prisoner. ²⁵For David said about him,

> 'I saw the Lord before me at all times;
> > he is by my right side, so that I will not
> > be troubled.
> ²⁶ Because of this my heart is glad
> > and my words are full of joy;
> > and I, mortal though I am,
> > will rest assured in hope,
> ²⁷ because you will not abandon my soul in
> > the world of the dead;
> > you will not allow your devoted servant
> > to suffer decay.
> ²⁸ You have shown me the paths that lead to
> > life,
> > and by your presence you will fill me
> > with joy.'

²⁹"Brothers: I must speak to you quite plainly about our patriarch David. He died and was buried, and his grave is here with us to this very day. ³⁰He was a prophet, and he knew God's promise to him: God made a vow that he would make one of David's descendants a king, just as David was. ³¹David saw what God was going to do, and so he spoke about the resurrection of the Messiah when he said,

> 'He was not abandoned in the world of the
> > dead;
> his flesh did not decay.'

³²God has raised this very Jesus from the dead, and we are all witnesses to this fact. ³³He has been raised to the right side of God and received from him the Holy Spirit, as his Father had promised; and what you now see and hear is his gift that he has poured out on us. ³⁴For David himself did not go up into heaven; rather he said,

> 'The Lord said to my Lord:
> > Sit here at my right side,

³⁵ until I put your enemies as a footstool
    under your feet.'

³⁶"All the people of Israel, then, are to know for sure
that it is this Jesus, whom you nailed to the cross, that
God has made Lord and Messiah!"

³⁷When the people heard this, they were deeply
troubled, and said to Peter and the other apostles,
"What shall we do, brothers?"

³⁸Peter said to them, "Turn away from your sins,
each one of you, and be baptized in the name of Jesus
Christ, so that your sins will be forgiven; and you will
receive God's gift, the Holy Spirit. ³⁹For God's promise was made to you and your children, and to all who
are far away—all whom the Lord our God calls to
himself."

⁴⁰Peter made his appeal to them and with many
other words he urged them, saying, "Save yourselves
from the punishment coming to this wicked people!"
⁴¹Many of them believed his message and were bap-
tized; about three thousand people were added to the
group that day. ⁴²They spent their time in learning
from the apostles, taking part in the fellowship, and
sharing in the fellowship meals and the prayers.

Life among the Believers

⁴³Many miracles and wonders were done through the
apostles, and this caused everyone to be filled with awe.
⁴⁴All the believers continued together in close fellow-
ship and shared their belongings with one another.
⁴⁵They would sell their property and possessions and
distribute the money among all, according to what each
one needed. ⁴⁶Every day they continued to meet as a
group in the temple, and they had their meals together
in their homes, eating the food with glad and humble
hearts, ⁴⁷praising God and enjoying the good will of all
the people. And every day the Lord added to their group
those who were being saved.

The Lame Man Healed

3   One day Peter and John went to the temple at three
    o'clock in the afternoon, the hour for prayers.
²There, at the "Beautiful Gate," as it was called, was a

He looked at them, expecting to get something

man who had been lame all his life. Every day he was carried to this gate to beg for money from the people who were going into the temple. ³When he saw Peter and John going in, he begged them to give him something. ⁴They looked straight at him and Peter said, "Look at us!" ⁵So he looked at them, expecting to get something from them. ⁶Peter said to him, "I have no money at all, but I will give you what I have: in the name of Jesus Christ of Nazareth I order you to walk!" ⁷Then he took him by his right hand and helped him up. At once the man's feet and ankles became strong; ⁸he jumped up, stood on his feet, and started walking around. Then he went into the temple with them, walking and jumping and praising God. ⁹The whole crowd saw him walking and praising God; ¹⁰and when they recognized him as the beggar who sat at the temple's "Beautiful Gate," they were all filled with surprise and amazement at what had happened to him.

Peter's Message in the Temple

¹¹As the man held on to Peter and John, all the people were amazed and ran to them in "Solomon's Porch," as it was called. ¹²When Peter saw the people, he said to

them, "Men of Israel, why are you surprised at this, and
why do you stare at us? Do you think that it was by
means of our own power or godliness that we made this
man walk? [13]The God of Abraham, Isaac, and Jacob, the
God of our ancestors, has given divine glory to his Servant Jesus. You handed him over to the authorities, and
you rejected him in Pilate's presence, even after Pilate
had decided to set him free. [14]He was holy and good, but
you rejected him and instead you asked Pilate to do you
the favour of turning loose a murderer. [15]And so you
killed the one who leads men to life. But God raised him
from the dead—and we are witnesses to this. [16]It was the
power of his name that gave strength to this lame man.
What you see and know was done by faith in his name;
it was faith in Jesus that made him well like this before
you all.

[17]"And now, my brothers, I know that what you and
your leaders did to Jesus was done because of your
ignorance. [18]God long ago announced by means of all
the prophets that his Messiah had to suffer; and he
made it come true in this way. [19]Repent, then, and
turn to God, so that he will wipe away your sins, [20]so
that times of spiritual strength may come from the
Lord's presence, and that he may send Jesus, who is
the Messiah he has already chosen for you. [21]He must
remain in heaven until the time comes for all things to
be made new, as God announced by means of his holy
prophets of long ago. [22]For Moses said, 'The Lord
your God will send you a prophet, just as he sent me,
who will be of your own people. You must listen to
everything that he tells you. [23]Anyone who does not
listen to what that prophet says will be separated from
God's people and destroyed.' [24]And the prophets, including Samuel and those who came after him, all of
them who had a message, also announced these present days. [25]The promises of God through his prophets
are for you, and you share in the covenant which God
made with your ancestors. As he said to Abraham,
'Through your descendants I will bless all the people
on earth.' [26]And so God chose and sent his Servant to
you first, to bless you by making all of you turn away
from your wicked ways."

Peter and John before the Council

4 Peter and John were still speaking to the people when the priests, the officer in charge of the temple guards, and the Sadducees came to them. [2]They were annoyed because the two apostles were teaching the people that Jesus had risen from death, which proved that the dead will rise to life. [3]So they arrested them and put them in jail until the next day, since it was already late. [4]But many who heard the message believed; and the number of men came to about five thousand.

[5]The next day the Jewish leaders, the elders, and the teachers of the Law gathered in Jerusalem. [6]They met with the High Priest Annas, and Caiaphas, and John, and Alexander, and the others who belonged to the High Priest's family. [7]They made the apostles stand before them and asked them, "How did you do this? What power do you have, or whose name did you use?"

[8]Peter, full of the Holy Spirit, answered them, "Leaders of the people and elders: [9]if we are being questioned today about the good deed done to the lame man and how he was made well, [10]then you should all know, and all the people of Israel should know, that this man stands here before you completely well by the power of the name of Jesus Christ of Nazareth—whom you crucified and God raised from death. [11]Jesus is the one of whom the scripture says,

'The stone that you the builders despised
    turned out to be the most important
    stone.'

[12]Salvation is to be found through him alone; for there is no one else in all the world, whose name God has given to men, by whom we can be saved."

[13]The members of the Council were amazed to see how bold Peter and John were, and to learn that they were ordinary men of no education. They realized then that they had been companions of Jesus. [14]But there was nothing that they could say, because they saw the man who had been made well standing there with Peter and John. [15]So they told them to leave the Council room, and started discussing among themselves. [16]"What shall we do with these men?" they asked.

"Everyone living in Jerusalem knows that this extraordinary miracle has been performed by them, and we cannot deny it. [17]But to keep this matter from spreading any further among the people, let us warn these men never again to speak to anyone in the name of Jesus."

[18]So they called them back in and told them that under no condition were they to speak or to teach in the name of Jesus. [19]But Peter and John answered them, "You yourselves judge which is right in God's sight, to obey you or to obey God. [20]For we cannot stop speaking of what we ourselves have seen and heard." [21]The Council warned them even more strongly, and then set them free. They could find no reason for punishing them, because the people were all praising God for what had happened. [22]The man on whom this miracle of healing had been performed was over forty years old.

The Believers Pray for Boldness

[23]As soon as they were set free, Peter and John returned to their group and told them what the chief priests and the elders had said. [24]When they heard it, they all joined together in prayer to God: "Master and Creator of heaven, earth, and sea, and all that is in them! [25]By means of the Holy Spirit you spoke through our ancestor David, your servant, when he said,

'Why were the Gentiles furious;
    why did the peoples plot in vain?
[26] The kings of the earth prepared themselves,
    and the rulers met together
    against the Lord and his Messiah.'

[27]For indeed Herod and Pontius Pilate met together in this city with the Gentiles and the people of Israel against Jesus, your holy Servant, whom you made Messiah. [28]They gathered to do everything that you, by your power and will, had already decided would take place. [29]And now, Lord, take notice of the threats they made and allow us, your servants, to speak your message with all boldness. [30]Stretch out your hand to heal, and grant that wonders and miracles may be performed through the name of your holy Servant Jesus."

[31]When they finished praying, the place where they were meeting was shaken. They were all filled with the Holy Spirit and began to speak God's message with boldness.

All Things Together

[32]The group of believers was one in mind and heart. No one said that any of his belongings was his own, but they all shared with one another everything they had. [33]With great power the apostles gave witness of the resurrection of the Lord Jesus, and God poured rich blessings on them all. [34]There was no one in the group who was in need. Those who owned fields or houses would sell them, bring the money received from the sale [35]and turn it over to the apostles; and the money was distributed to each one according to his need.

[36]And so it was that Joseph, a Levite born in Cyprus, whom the apostles called Barnabas (which means "One who Encourages"), [37]sold a field he owned, brought the money and turned it over to the apostles.

Ananias and Sapphira

5 But there was a man named Ananias, whose wife was named Sapphira. He sold some property that belonged to them, [2]but kept part of the money for himself, as his wife knew, and turned the rest over to the apostles. [3]Peter said to him, "Ananias, why did you let Satan take control of your heart and make you lie to the Holy Spirit by keeping part of the money you received for the property? [4]Before you sold the property it belonged to you, and after you sold it the money was yours. Why, then, did you decide in your heart that you would do such a thing? You have not lied to men—you have lied to God!" [5]As soon as Ananias heard this he fell down dead; and all who heard about it were filled with fear. [6]The young men came in, wrapped up his body, took him out and buried him.

[7]About three hours later his wife came in, but she did not know what had happened. [8]Peter said to her, "Tell me, was this the full amount you and your husband received for your property?"

"Yes," she answered, "the full amount."

⁹So Peter said to her, "Why did you and your husband decide to put the Lord's Spirit to the test? The men who buried your husband are at the door right now, and they will carry you out too!" ¹⁰At once she fell down at his feet and died. The young men came in and saw that she was dead, so they carried her out and buried her beside her husband. ¹¹The whole church and all the others who heard of this were filled with great fear.

Miracles and Wonders

¹²Many miracles and wonders were being performed among the people by the apostles. All the believers met together in a group in Solomon's Porch. ¹³Nobody outside the group dared join them, even though the people spoke highly of them. ¹⁴But more and more people were added to the group—a crowd of men and women who believed in the Lord. ¹⁵As a result of what the apostles were doing, the sick people were carried out in the streets and placed on beds and mats so that, when Peter walked by, at least his shadow might fall on some of them. ¹⁶And crowds of people came in from the towns round Jerusalem, bringing their sick and those who had evil spirits in them; and they were all healed.

The Apostles Persecuted

¹⁷Then the High Priest and all his companions, members of the local party of the Sadducees, became extremely jealous of the apostles; so they decided to take action. ¹⁸They arrested the apostles and placed them in the public jail. ¹⁹But that night an angel of the Lord opened the prison gates, led the apostles out, and said to them, ²⁰"Go and stand in the temple, and tell the people all about this new life." ²¹The apostles obeyed, and at dawn they entered the temple and started teaching.

The High Priest and his companions called together all the Jewish elders for a full meeting of the Council; then they sent orders to the prison to have the apostles brought before them. ²²But when the officials arrived, they did not find the apostles in prison; so they returned to the Council and reported, ²³"When we arrived at the jail we found it locked up tight and all the guards on

Listen!

watch at the gates; but when we opened the gates we did not find anyone inside!" ²⁴When the officer in charge of the temple guards and the chief priests heard this, they wondered what had happened to the apostles. ²⁵Then a man came in who said to them, "Listen! The men you put in prison are standing in the temple teaching the people!" ²⁶So the officer went off with his men and brought the apostles back. They did not use force, however, because they were afraid that the people might stone them.

²⁷They brought the apostles in and made them stand before the Council, and the High Priest questioned them. ²⁸"We gave you strict orders not to teach in the name of this man," he said; "but see what you have done! You have spread your teaching all over Jerusalem, and you want to make us responsible for his death!"

²⁹Peter and the other apostles answered back, "We must obey God, not men. ³⁰The God of our fathers raised Jesus from death, after you had killed him by nailing him to a cross. ³¹God raised him to his right side as Leader and Saviour, to give to the people of Israel the opportunity to repent and have their sins forgiven. ³²We are witnesses to these things—we and the Holy Spirit, who is God's gift to those who obey him."

³³When the members of the Council heard this they were so furious that they decided to have the apostles put to death. ³⁴But one of them, a Pharisee named

Gamaliel, a teacher of the Law who was highly respected by all the people, stood up in the Council. He
ordered the apostles to be taken out, [35]and then said to
the Council, "Men of Israel, be careful what you are
about to do to these men. [36]Some time ago Theudas
appeared, claiming that he was somebody great; and
about four hundred men joined him. But he was killed,
all his followers were scattered, and his movement
died out. [37]After this, Judas the Galilean appeared during the time of the census; he also drew a crowd after
him, but he also was killed and all his followers were
scattered. [38]And so in this case now, I tell you, do not
take any action against these men. Leave them alone,
because if this plan and work of theirs is a man-made
thing, it will disappear; [39]but if it comes from God you
cannot possibly defeat them. You could find yourselves fighting against God!"

The Council followed Gamaliel's advice. [40]They
called the apostles in, had them whipped, and ordered
them never again to speak in the name of Jesus; and
then they set them free. [41]The apostles left the Council, full of joy that God had considered them worthy to
suffer disgrace for the name of Jesus. [42]And every day
in the temple and in people's homes they continued to
teach and preach the Good News about Jesus the Messiah.

The Seven Helpers

6   Some time later, as the number of disciples kept
    growing, there was a quarrel between the Greek-
speaking Jews and the native Jews. The Greek-speaking
Jews said that their widows were being neglected in the
daily distribution of funds. [2]So the twelve apostles called
the whole group of disciples together and said, "It is not
right for us to neglect the preaching of God's word in
order to handle finances. [3]So then, brothers, choose
seven men among you who are known to be full of the
Holy Spirit and wisdom, and we will put them in charge
of this matter. [4]We ourselves, then, will give our full
time to prayers and the work of preaching."

[5]The whole group was pleased with the apostles'
proposal; so they chose Stephen, a man full of faith and

the Holy Spirit, and Philip, Prochorus, Nicanor, Timon, Parmenas, and Nicolaus, a Gentile from Antioch who had been converted to Judaism. ⁶The group presented them to the apostles, who prayed and placed their hands on them.

⁷And so the word of God continued to spread. The number of disciples in Jerusalem grew larger and larger, and a great number of priests accepted the faith.

The Arrest of Stephen

⁸Stephen, a man richly blessed by God and full of power, performed great miracles and wonders among the people. ⁹But some men opposed him; they were members of the synagogue of the Free Men (as it was called), which had Jews from Cyrenia and Alexandria. They and other Jews from Cilicia and Asia started arguing with Stephen. ¹⁰But the Spirit gave Stephen such wisdom that when he spoke they could not resist him. ¹¹So they bribed some men to say, "We heard him speaking against Moses and against God!" ¹²In this way they stirred up the people, the elders, and the teachers of the Law. They came to Stephen, seized him, and took him before the Council. ¹³Then they brought in some men to tell lies about him. "This man," they said, "is always talking against our sacred temple and the Law of Moses. ¹⁴We heard him say that this Jesus of Nazareth will tear down the temple and change all the customs which have come down to us from Moses!" ¹⁵All those sitting in the Council fixed their eyes on Stephen and saw that his face looked like the face of an angel.

Stephen's Speech

7 The High Priest asked Stephen, "Is this really so?" ²Stephen answered, "Brothers and fathers! Listen to me! The God of glory appeared to our ancestor Abraham while he was living in Mesopotamia, before he had gone to live in Haran, ³and said to him, 'Leave your family and country and go to the land that I will show you.' ⁴And so he left the land of Chaldea and went to live in Haran. After Abraham's father died, God made him move to this country, where you now live. ⁵God did not then give Abraham any part of it as his own, not even a square foot of ground; but God promised that he

would give it to him, and that it would belong to him and his descendants after him. At the time God made this promise Abraham had no children. ⁶This is what God said to him, 'Your descendants will live in a foreign country, where they will be slaves and will be badly treated for four hundred years. ⁷But I will pass judgment on the people that they will serve,' God said, 'and afterwards they will come out of that country and will worship me in this place.' ⁸Then God gave to Abraham the ceremony of circumcision as a sign of the covenant. So Abraham circumcised Isaac a week after he was born; Isaac circumcised Jacob, and Jacob circumcised the twelve patriarchs.

⁹"The patriarchs were jealous of Joseph, and sold him to be a slave in Egypt. But God was with him, ¹⁰and brought him safely through all his troubles. When Joseph appeared before Pharaoh, the king of Egypt, God gave him a pleasing manner and wisdom. Pharaoh made Joseph governor over the country and the royal household. ¹¹Then there was a famine in all of Egypt and Canaan, which caused much suffering. Our ancestors could not find any food. ¹²So when Jacob heard that there was grain in Egypt, he sent his sons, our ancestors, on their first visit there. ¹³On the second visit Joseph made himself known to his brothers, and Pharaoh came to know about Joseph's family. ¹⁴So Joseph sent a message to his father Jacob, telling him and the whole family to come to Egypt; there were seventy-five people in all. ¹⁵Then Jacob went down to Egypt, where he and our ancestors died. ¹⁶Their bodies were moved to Shechem, where they were buried in the grave which Abraham had bought from the tribe of Hamor for a sum of money.

¹⁷"When the time drew near for God to keep the promise he had made to Abraham, the number of our people in Egypt had grown much larger. ¹⁸At last a different king, who had not known Joseph, began to rule in Egypt. ¹⁹He tricked our people and was cruel to our ancestors, forcing them to put their babies out of their homes, so that they would die. ²⁰It was at this time that Moses was born, a very beautiful child. He was brought up at home for three months, ²¹and when he was put out of his home the daughter of Pharaoh

adopted him and brought him up as her own son. ²²He was taught all the wisdom of the Egyptians, and became a great man in words and deeds.

²³"When Moses was forty years old he decided to visit his fellow Israelites. ²⁴He saw one of them being mistreated by an Egyptian; so he went to his help and took revenge on the Egyptian by killing him. ²⁵(He thought that his own people would understand that God was going to use him to set them free; but they did not understand.) ²⁶The next day he saw two Israelites fighting, and he tried to make peace between them. 'Listen, men,' he said, 'you are brothers; why do you mistreat each other?' ²⁷But the one who was mistreating the other pushed Moses aside. 'Who made you ruler and judge over us?' he asked. ²⁸'Do you want to kill me, just as you killed that Egyptian yesterday?' ²⁹When Moses heard this he fled from Egypt and started living in the land of Midian. There he had two sons.

³⁰"After forty years had passed, an angel appeared to Moses in the flames of a burning bush in the desert near Mount Sinai. ³¹Moses was amazed by what he saw, and went near the bush to look at it closely. But he heard the Lord's voice: ³²'I am the God of your ancestors, the God of Abraham, Isaac, and Jacob.' Moses trembled with fear and dared not look. ³³The Lord said to him, 'Take your sandals off, for the place where you are standing is holy ground. ³⁴I have looked and seen the cruel suffering of my people in Egypt. I have heard their groans, and I have come down to save them. Come now, I will send you to Egypt.'

³⁵"Moses is the one who was rejected by the people of Israel. 'Who made you ruler and judge over us?' they asked. He is the one whom God sent as ruler and saviour, with the help of the angel who appeared to him in the burning bush. ³⁶He led the people out of Egypt, performing miracles and wonders in Egypt and the Red Sea, and in the desert for forty years. ³⁷Moses is the one who said to the people of Israel, 'God will send you a prophet, just as he sent me, who will be of your own people.' ³⁸He is the one who was with the people of Israel assembled in the desert; he was there with our ancestors and with the angel who spoke to

him on Mount Sinai; he received God's living messages to pass on to us.

³⁹"But our ancestors refused to obey him; they pushed him aside and wished that they could go back to Egypt. ⁴⁰So they said to Aaron, 'Make us some gods who will go in front of us. We do not know what has happened to that Moses who brought us out of Egypt.' ⁴¹It was then that they made an idol in the shape of a calf, offered sacrifice to it, and had a feast to celebrate what they themselves had made. ⁴²But God turned away from them, and gave them over to worship the stars of heaven, as it is written in the book of the prophets,

> 'People of Israel! It was not to me
>   that you slaughtered and sacrificed
>   animals
>   for forty years in the desert.
> ⁴³ It was the tent of the god Moloch that
>   you carried,
>   and the image of the star of your god
>   Rephan;
>   they were idols that you had made to
>   worship.
> And so I will send you away beyond
>   Babylon.'

⁴⁴"Our ancestors had the tent of God's presence with them in the desert. It had been made as God had told Moses to make it, according to the pattern that Moses had been shown. ⁴⁵Later on, our ancestors who received the tent from their fathers carried it with them when they went with Joshua and took over the land from the nations that God drove out before them. And it stayed there until the time of David. ⁴⁶He won God's favour, and asked God to allow him to provide a house for the God of Jacob. ⁴⁷But it was Solomon who built him a house.

⁴⁸"But the Most High God does not live in houses built by men; as the prophet says,

> ⁴⁹ 'Heaven is my throne, says the Lord,
>   and earth is my footstool.
> What kind of house would you build for
>   me?
> Where is the place for me to rest?

⁵⁰ Did not I myself make all these things?'
⁵¹"How stubborn you are! How heathen your hearts, how deaf you are to God's message! You are just like your ancestors: you too have always resisted the Holy Spirit! ⁵²Was there any prophet that your ancestors did not persecute? They killed God's messengers, who long ago announced the coming of his righteous Servant. And now you have betrayed and murdered him. ⁵³You are the ones who received God's law, that was handed down by angels—yet you have not obeyed it!"

The Stoning of Stephen

⁵⁴As the members of the Council listened to Stephen they became furious and ground their teeth at him in anger. ⁵⁵But Stephen, full of the Holy Spirit, looked up to heaven and saw God's glory, and Jesus standing at the right side of God. ⁵⁶"Look!" he said. "I see heaven opened and the Son of Man standing at the right side of God!"

They threw him out of the city and stoned him

⁵⁷With a loud cry they covered their ears with their hands. Then they all rushed together at him at once, ⁵⁸threw him out of the city and stoned him. The witnesses left their cloaks in charge of a young man named Saul. ⁵⁹They kept on stoning Stephen as he called on the Lord, "Lord Jesus, receive my spirit!" ⁶⁰He knelt down and cried out in a loud voice, "Lord! Do not remember this sin against them!" He said this and died.

8 And Saul approved of his murder.

Saul Persecutes the Church

That very day the church in Jerusalem began to suffer cruel persecution. All the believers, except the apostles, were scattered throughout the provinces of Judea and Samaria. ²Some devout men buried Stephen, mourning for him with loud cries.

³But Saul tried to destroy the church; going from house to house, he dragged out the believers, both men and women, and threw them into jail.

The Gospel Preached in Samaria

⁴The believers who were scattered went everywhere, preaching the message. ⁵Philip went to the city of Samaria and preached the Messiah to the people there. ⁶The crowds paid close attention to what Philip said. They all listened to him and saw the miracles that he performed. ⁷Evil spirits came out with a loud cry from many people; many paralysed and lame people were also healed. ⁸So there was great joy in Samaria.

⁹In that city lived a man named Simon, who for some time had astounded the Samaritans with his magic. He claimed that he was someone great, ¹⁰and everyone in the city, from all classes of society, paid close attention to him. "He is that power of God known as 'The Great Power,'" they said. ¹¹He had astounded them with his magic for such a long time that they paid close attention to him. ¹²But when they believed Philip's message about the Good News of the Kingdom of God and the name of Jesus Christ, they were baptized, both men and women. ¹³Simon himself also believed; and after being baptized he stayed close to Philip, and was astounded when he saw the great wonders and miracles that were being performed.

¹⁴The apostles in Jerusalem heard that the people of Samaria had received the word of God; so they sent Peter and John to them. ¹⁵When they arrived, they prayed for the believers that they might receive the Holy Spirit. ¹⁶For the Holy Spirit had not yet come down on any of them; they had only been baptized in the name of the Lord Jesus. ¹⁷Then Peter and John placed their hands on them, and they received the Holy Spirit.

¹⁸Simon saw that the Spirit had been given to them when the apostles placed their hands on them. So he offered money to Peter and John, ¹⁹and said, "Give this power to me too, so that anyone I place my hands on will receive the Holy Spirit."

²⁰But Peter answered him, "May you and your money go to hell, for thinking that you can buy God's gift with money! ²¹You have no part or share in our work, because your heart is not right in God's sight. ²²Repent, then, from this evil plan of yours, and pray to the Lord that he will forgive you for thinking such a thing as this. ²³For I see that you are full of bitter envy, and are a prisoner of sin."

²⁴Simon said to Peter and John, "Please pray to the Lord for me, so that none of these things you said will happen to me."

²⁵After they had given their testimony and spoken the Lord's message, Peter and John went back to Jerusalem. On their way they preached the Good News in many villages of Samaria.

Philip and the Ethiopian Official

²⁶An angel of the Lord spoke to Philip, "Get yourself ready and go south to the road that goes from Jerusalem to Gaza." (This road is no longer used.) ²⁷⁻²⁸So Philip got ready and went. Now an Ethiopian eunuch was on his way home. This man was an important official in charge of the treasury of the Queen, or Candace, of Ethiopia. He had been to Jerusalem to worship God, and was going back in his carriage. As he rode along he was reading from the book of the prophet Isaiah. ²⁹The Holy Spirit said to Philip, "Go over and stay close to that carriage." ³⁰Philip ran over and heard him reading

from the book of the prophet Isaiah; so he asked him,
"Do you understand what you are reading?"
³¹"How can I understand," the official replied, "unless someone explains it to me?" And he invited Philip
to climb up and sit in the carriage with him. ³²The
passage of scripture which he was reading was this,

> "He was like a sheep that is taken to be
>   slaughtered;
>   he was like a lamb that makes no
>   sound when its wool is cut off;
>   he did not say a word.
> ³³ He was humiliated, and justice was de-
>   nied him.
> No one will be able to tell about his de-
>   scendants,
>   because his life on earth has come to
>   an end."

³⁴The official said to Philip, "Tell me, of whom is the
prophet saying this? Of himself or of someone else?"
³⁵Philip began to speak; starting from this very passage
of scripture, he told him the Good News about Jesus.
³⁶As they travelled down the road they came to a
place where there was some water, and the official
said, "Here is some water. What is to keep me from
being baptized?"
    [³⁷Philip said to him, "You may be baptized if you
believe with all your heart."
    "I do," he answered; "I believe that Jesus Christ is
the Son of God."]
³⁸The official ordered the carriage to stop; and both
of them, Philip and the official, went down into the
water, and Philip baptized him. ³⁹When they came up
out of the water the Spirit of the Lord took Philip
away. The official did not see him again, but continued
on his way, full of joy. ⁴⁰Philip found himself in Ash-
dod; and he went through all the towns preaching the
Good News, until he arrived at Caesarea.

The Conversion of Saul
(Also Acts 22.6–16; 26.12–18)

9 In the meantime Saul kept up his violent threats of
    murder against the disciples of the Lord. He went
to the High Priest ²and asked for letters of introduction

to the Jewish synagogues in Damascus, so that if he should find any followers of the Way of the Lord there, he would be able to arrest them, both men and women, and take them back to Jerusalem.

He fell to the ground

³On his way to Damascus, as he came near the city, suddenly a light from the sky flashed round him. ⁴He fell to the ground and heard a voice saying to him, "Saul, Saul! Why do you persecute me?"

⁵"Who are you, Lord?" he asked.

"I am Jesus, whom you persecute," the voice said. ⁶"But get up and go into the city, where you will be told what you must do."

⁷The men who were travelling with Saul had stopped, not saying a word; they heard the voice but could not see anyone. ⁸Saul got up from the ground and opened his eyes, but could not see a thing. So they took him by the hand and led him into Damascus. ⁹For three days he

was not able to see, and during that time he did not eat or drink anything.

¹⁰There was a disciple in Damascus named Ananias. He had a vision, in which the Lord said to him, "Ananias!"

"Here I am, Lord," he answered.

¹¹The Lord said to him, "Get ready and go to Straight Street, and at the house of Judas ask for a man from Tarsus named Saul. He is praying, ¹²and in a vision he saw a man named Ananias come in and place his hands on him so that he might see again."

¹³Ananias answered, "Lord, many people have told me about this man, about all the terrible things he has done to your people in Jerusalem. ¹⁴And he has come to Damascus with authority from the chief priests to arrest all who call on your name."

¹⁵The Lord said to him, "Go, because I have chosen him to serve me, to make my name known to Gentiles and kings, and to the people of Israel. ¹⁶And I myself will show him all that he must suffer for my sake."

¹⁷So Ananias went, entered the house and placed his hands on Saul. "Brother Saul," he said, "the Lord has sent me—Jesus himself, who appeared to you on the road as you were coming here. He sent me so that you might see again and be filled with the Holy Spirit." ¹⁸At once something like fish scales fell from Saul's eyes and he was able to see again. He stood up and was baptized; ¹⁹and after he had eaten, his strength came back.

Saul Preaches in Damascus

Saul stayed for a few days with the disciples in Damascus. ²⁰He went straight to the synagogues and began to preach about Jesus. "He is the Son of God," he said.

²¹All who heard him were amazed, and asked, "Isn't this the man who in Jerusalem was killing those who call on this name? And didn't he come here for the very purpose of arresting them and taking them back to the chief priests?"

²²But Saul's preaching became even more powerful, and his proofs that Jesus was the Messiah were so con-

vincing that the Jews who lived in Damascus could not answer him.

²³After many days had gone by, the Jews gathered and made plans to kill Saul; ²⁴but he was told of what they planned to do. Day and night they watched the city gates in order to kill him. ²⁵But one night Saul's followers took him and let him down through an opening in the wall, lowering him in a basket.

Saul in Jerusalem

²⁶Saul went to Jerusalem and tried to join the disciples. They would not believe, however, that he was a disciple, and they were all afraid of him. ²⁷Then Barnabas came to his help and took him to the apostles. He explained to them how Saul had seen the Lord on the road, and that the Lord had spoken to him. He also told them how boldly Saul had preached in the name of Jesus in Damascus. ²⁸And so Saul stayed with them and went all over Jerusalem, preaching boldly in the name of the Lord. ²⁹He also talked and disputed with the Greek-speaking Jews, but they tried to kill him. ³⁰When the brothers found out about this, they took Saul down to Caesarea and sent him away to Tarsus.

³¹And so it was that the church throughout all of Judea, Galilee, and Samaria had a time of peace. It was built up and grew in numbers through the help of the Holy Spirit, as it lived in reverence for the Lord.

Peter in Lydda and Joppa

³²Peter travelled everywhere, and one time he went to visit God's people who lived in Lydda. ³³There he met a man named Aeneas, who was paralysed and had not been able to get out of bed for eight years. ³⁴"Aeneas," Peter said to him, "Jesus Christ makes you well. Get up and make your bed." At once Aeneas got up. ³⁵All the people living in Lydda and Sharon saw him, and they turned to the Lord.

³⁶In Joppa there was a woman named Tabitha, who was a believer. (Her name in Greek is Dorcas, meaning a deer.) She spent all her time doing good and helping the poor. ³⁷At that time she got sick and died. Her body

was washed and laid in a room upstairs. ³⁸Joppa was not very far from Lydda, and when the disciples in Joppa heard that Peter was in Lydda, they sent two men to him with the message, "Please hurry and come to us." ³⁹So Peter got ready and went with them. When he arrived he was taken to the room upstairs. All the widows crowded round him, crying and showing him the shirts and coats that Dorcas had made while she was alive. ⁴⁰Peter put them all out of the room, and knelt down and prayed; then he turned to the body and said, "Tabitha, get up!" She opened her eyes, and when she saw Peter she sat up. ⁴¹Peter reached over and helped her get up. Then he called the believers and the widows, and presented her alive to them. ⁴²The news about this spread all over Joppa, and many people believed in the Lord. ⁴³Peter stayed on in Joppa for many days with a leatherworker named Simon.

Peter and Cornelius

10 There was a man in Caesarea named Cornelius, a captain in the Roman army regiment called "The Italian Regiment." ²He was a religious man; he and his whole family worshipped God. He did much to help the Jewish poor people, and was constantly praying to God. ³It was about three o'clock one afternoon when he had a vision, in which he clearly saw an angel of God come in and say to him, "Cornelius!"

⁴He stared at the angel in fear and said, "What is it, sir?"

The angel answered, "God has accepted your prayers and works of charity, and has remembered you. ⁵And now send some men to Joppa to call for a certain man whose full name is Simon Peter. ⁶He is a guest in the home of a leatherworker named Simon, who lives by the sea." ⁷Then the angel who was speaking to him went away, and Cornelius called two of his house servants and a soldier, a religious man who was one of his personal attendants. ⁸He told them what had happened and sent them off to Joppa.

⁹The next day, as they were on their way and coming near Joppa, Peter went up on the roof of the house about noon in order to pray. ¹⁰He became hungry, and wanted

to eat; while the food was being prepared he had a vision. [11]He saw heaven opened and something coming down that looked like a large sheet being lowered by its four corners to the earth. [12]In it were all kinds of animals, reptiles, and wild birds. [13]A voice said to him, "Get up, Peter; kill and eat!"

[14]But Peter said, "Certainly not, Lord! I have never eaten anything considered defiled or unclean."

[15]The voice spoke to him again, "Do not consider anything unclean that God has declared clean." [16]This happened three times; and then the thing was taken back up into heaven.

[17]Peter was wondering about the meaning of this vision that he had seen. In the meantime the men sent by Cornelius had learned where Simon's house was, and were now standing in front of the gate. [18]They called out and asked, "Is there a guest here by the name of Simon Peter?"

[19]Peter was still trying to understand what the vision meant, when the Spirit said, "Listen! Three men are here looking for you. [20]So get yourself ready and go down, and do not hesitate to go with them, because I have sent them." [21]So Peter went down and said to the men, "I am the man you are looking for. Why have you come?"

[22]"Captain Cornelius sent us," they answered. "He is a good man who worships God and is highly respected by all the Jewish people. He was told by one of God's angels to invite you to his house, so that he could hear what you have to say." [23]Peter invited the men in and had them spend the night there.

The next day he got ready and went with them; and some of the brothers from Joppa went along with him. [24]The following day he arrived in Caesarea, where Cornelius was waiting for him, together with relatives and close friends that he had invited. [25]As Peter was about to go in, Cornelius met him, fell at his feet and bowed down before him. [26]But Peter made him rise. "Stand up," he said, "because I myself am only a man." [27]Peter kept on talking to Cornelius as he went into the house, where he found many people gathered. [28]He said to them, "You yourselves know very well

"Stand up," he said, "because I myself am only a man"

that a Jew is not allowed by his religion to visit or associate with a Gentile. But God has shown me that I must not consider any man unclean or defiled. ²⁹And so when you sent for me I came without any objection. I ask you, then, why did you send for me?"

³⁰Cornelius said, "It was about this time three days ago that I was praying in my house at three o'clock in the afternoon. Suddenly a man dressed in shining clothes stood in front of me ³¹and said: 'Cornelius! God has heard your prayer, and has remembered your works of charity. ³²Send someone to Joppa to call for a man whose full name is Simon Peter. He is a guest in the home of Simon the leatherworker, who lives by the sea.' ³³And so I sent for you at once, and you have been good enough to come. Now we are all here in the presence of God, waiting to hear anything that the Lord has ordered you to say."

Peter's Speech

³⁴Peter began to speak: "I now realize that it is true that God treats all men on the same basis. ³⁵Whoever fears him and does what is right is acceptable to him, no matter what race he belongs to. ³⁶You know the message he sent to the people of Israel, proclaiming the Good News of peace through Jesus Christ, who is Lord of all men. ³⁷You know of the great event that took place throughout all the land of Israel, beginning in Galilee, after the baptism that John preached. ³⁸You know about

Jesus of Nazareth, how God poured out on him the Holy Spirit and power. He went everywhere, doing good and healing all who were under the power of the Devil, because God was with him. ³⁹We are witnesses of all that he did in the country of the Jews and in Jerusalem. They put him to death by nailing him to the cross. ⁴⁰But God raised him from death on the third day, and caused him to appear, ⁴¹not to all the people, but only to us who are the witnesses that God had already chosen. We ate and drank with him after he rose from death. ⁴²And he commanded us to preach the gospel to the people, and to testify that he is the one whom God has appointed judge of the living and the dead. ⁴³All the prophets spoke about him, saying that everyone who believes in him will have his sins forgiven through the power of his name."

The Gentiles Receive the Holy Spirit

⁴⁴While Peter was still speaking, the Holy Spirit came down on all those who were listening to the message. ⁴⁵The Jewish believers who had come from Joppa with Peter were amazed that God had poured out his gift of the Holy Spirit on the Gentiles also. ⁴⁶For they heard them speaking in strange tongues and praising God's greatness. Peter spoke up, ⁴⁷"These people have received the Holy Spirit, just as we also did. Can anyone, then, stop them from being baptized with water?" ⁴⁸So he ordered them to be baptized in the name of Jesus Christ. Then they asked him to stay with them for a few days.

Peter's Report to the Church at Jerusalem

11 The apostles and the brothers throughout all of Judea heard that the Gentiles also had received the word of God. ²When Peter went up to Jerusalem, those who were in favour of circumcising Gentiles criticized him, ³"You were a guest in the home of uncircumcised Gentiles, and you even ate with them!" ⁴So Peter gave them a full account of what had happened, from the very beginning:

⁵"I was praying in the city of Joppa, and I had a vision. I saw something coming down that looked like a large

sheet being lowered by its four corners from heaven, and it stopped next to me. ⁶I looked closely inside and saw animals, beasts, reptiles, and wild birds. ⁷Then I heard a voice saying to me, 'Get up, Peter; kill and eat!' ⁸But I said, 'Certainly not, Lord! No defiled or unclean food has ever entered my mouth.' ⁹The voice spoke again from heaven, 'Do not consider anything unclean that God has declared clean.' ¹⁰This happened three times, and finally the whole thing was drawn back up into heaven. ¹¹At that very moment three men who had been sent to me from Caesarea arrived at the house where I was staying. ¹²The Spirit told me to go with them without hesitation. These six brothers from Joppa also went with me to Caesarea, and we all went into the house of Cornelius. ¹³He told us how he had seen an angel standing in his house who said to him, 'Send someone to Joppa to call for a man whose full name is Simon Peter. ¹⁴He will speak words to you by which you and all your family will be saved.' ¹⁵And when I began to speak, the Holy Spirit came down on them just as on us at the beginning. ¹⁶Then I remembered what the Lord had said, 'John baptized with water, but you will be baptized with the Holy Spirit.' ¹⁷It is clear that God gave those Gentiles the same gift that he gave us when we believed in the Lord Jesus Christ; who was I, then, to try to stop God!''

¹⁸When they heard this, they stopped their criticism and praised God, saying, "Then God has given to the Gentiles also the opportunity to repent and live!"

The Church at Antioch

¹⁹The believers were scattered by the persecution which took place when Stephen was killed. Some of them went as far as Phoenicia and Cyprus and Antioch, telling the message to Jews only. ²⁰But some of the believers, men from Cyprus and Cyrene, went to Antioch and proclaimed the message to Gentiles also, telling them the Good News about the Lord Jesus. ²¹The Lord's power was with them, and a great number of people believed and turned to the Lord.

²²The news about this reached the church in Jerusalem, so they sent Barnabas to Antioch. ²³When he

arrived and saw how God had blessed the people, he was glad and urged them all to be faithful and true to the Lord with all their hearts. 24Barnabas was a good man, full of the Holy Spirit and faith. Many people were brought to the Lord.

25Then Barnabas went to Tarsus to look for Saul. 26When he found him, he brought him to Antioch. For a whole year the two met with the people of the church and taught a large group. It was at Antioch that the disciples were first called Christians.

27About that time some prophets went down from Jerusalem to Antioch. 28One of them, named Agabus, stood up and by the power of the Spirit predicted that a great famine was about to come over all the earth. (It came when Claudius was Emperor.) 29The disciples decided that each of them would send as much as he could to help their brothers who lived in Judea. 30They did this, then, and sent the money to the church elders by Barnabas and Saul.

More Persecution

12 About this time King Herod began to persecute some members of the church. 2He had James, the brother of John, put to death by the sword. 3When he saw that this pleased the Jews, he went ahead and had Peter arrested. (This happened during the time of the Feast of Unleavened Bread.) 4After his arrest Peter was put in jail, where he was handed over to be guarded by four groups of four soldiers each. Herod planned to put him on trial in public after Passover. 5So Peter was kept in jail, but the people of the church were praying earnestly to God for him.

Peter Set Free from Prison

6The night before Herod was going to bring him out to the people, Peter was sleeping between two guards. He was tied with two chains, and there were guards on duty at the prison gate. 7Suddenly an angel of the Lord stood there, and a light shone in the cell. The angel shook Peter by the shoulder, woke him up and said, "Hurry! Get up!" At once the chains fell off Peter's hands. 8Then the angel said, "Tighten your belt and tie

Peter was sleeping between two guards

on your sandals." Peter did so, and the angel said, "Put your cloak round you and come with me." ⁹Peter followed him out of the prison. He did not know, however, if what the angel was doing was real; he thought he was seeing a vision. ¹⁰They passed by the first guard station, and then the second, and came at last to the iron gate that opens into the city. The gate opened for them by itself, and they went out. They walked down a street, and suddenly the angel left Peter.

¹¹Then Peter realized what had happened to him, and said, "Now I know that it is really true! The Lord sent his angel, and he rescued me from Herod's power and from all the things the Jewish people expected to do."

¹²Aware of his situation, he went to the home of Mary, the mother of John Mark. Many people had gathered there and were praying. ¹³Peter knocked at the outside door, and a servant girl named Rhoda came to answer it. ¹⁴She recognized Peter's voice and was so happy that she ran back in without opening the door, and announced that Peter was standing outside. ¹⁵"You are crazy!" they told her. But she insisted that it was true. So they answered, "It is his angel."

¹⁶Meanwhile, Peter kept on knocking. They opened the door at last and when they saw him they were amazed. ¹⁷He motioned with his hand for them to be quiet, and explained to them how the Lord had brought him out of prison. "Tell this to James and the rest of the brothers," he said; then he left and went somewhere else.

¹⁸When morning came, there was a tremendous confusion among the guards; what had happened to Peter? ¹⁹Herod gave orders to search for him, but they could not find him. So he had the guards questioned and ordered them to be put to death.

After this Herod went down from Judea and spent some time in Caesarea.

The Death of Herod

²⁰Herod was very angry with the people of Tyre and Sidon; so they went in a group to see Herod. First they won Blastus over to their side; he was in charge of the palace. Then they went to Herod and asked him for peace, because their country got its food supplies from the king's country.

²¹On a chosen day Herod put on his royal robes, sat on his throne, and made a speech to the people. ²²"It isn't a man speaking, but a god!" they shouted. ²³At once the angel of the Lord struck Herod down, because he did not give honour to God. He was eaten by worms and died.

²⁴The word of God continued to spread and grow.

²⁵Barnabas and Saul finished their mission and returned from Jerusalem, taking John Mark with them.

Barnabas and Saul Chosen and Sent

13 In the church at Antioch there were some prophets and teachers: Barnabas, Simeon (called the Black), Lucius (from Cyrene), Manaen (who had been brought up with Governor Herod), and Saul. ²While they were serving the Lord and fasting, the Holy Spirit said to them, "Set apart for me Barnabas and Saul, to do the work to which I have called them."

³They fasted and prayed, placed their hands on them and sent them off.

In Cyprus

⁴Barnabas and Saul, then, having been sent by the Holy Spirit, went down to Seleucia and sailed from there to the island of Cyprus. ⁵When they arrived at Salamis, they preached the word of God in the Jewish synagogues. They had John Mark with them to help in the work.

⁶They went all the way across the island to Paphos, where they met a certain magician named Bar-Jesus, a Jew who claimed to be a prophet. ⁷He was a friend of the Governor of the island, Sergius Paulus, who was an intelligent man. The Governor called Barnabas and Saul before him because he wanted to hear the word of God. ⁸But they were opposed by the magician Elymas (this is his name in Greek); he tried to turn the Governor away from the faith. ⁹Then Saul—also known as Paul—was filled with the Holy Spirit; he looked straight at the magician ¹⁰and said, "You son of the Devil! You are the enemy of everything that is good; you are full of all kinds of evil tricks, and you always keep trying to turn the Lord's truths into lies! ¹¹The Lord's hand will come down on you now; you will be blind, and will not see the light of day for a time."

At once Elymas felt a black mist cover his eyes, and he walked around trying to find someone to lead him by the hand. ¹²The Governor believed when he saw what had happened; he was greatly amazed at the teaching about the Lord.

In Antioch of Pisidia

¹³Paul and his companions sailed from Paphos and came to Perga, in Pamphylia; but John Mark left them there and went back to Jerusalem. ¹⁴They went on from Perga and came to Antioch of Pisidia; and on the Sabbath day they went into the synagogue and sat down. ¹⁵After the reading from the Law of Moses and the writings of the prophets, the officials of the synagogue sent them a message: "Brothers, we want you to speak to the people if you have a message of encouragement for them." ¹⁶Paul stood up, motioned with his hand, and began to speak:

"Fellow Israelites and all Gentiles here who worship

God: hear me! [17]The God of this people of Israel chose
our ancestors, and made the people a great nation during the time they lived as foreigners in the land of Egypt.
God brought them out of Egypt by his great power,
[18]and for forty years he endured them in the desert. [19]He
destroyed seven nations in the land of Canaan and made
his people the owners of the land [20]for about four hundred and fifty years.

"After this he gave them judges, until the time of
the prophet Samuel. [21]And when they asked for a king,
God gave them Saul, the son of Kish, from the tribe of
Benjamin, to be their king for forty years. [22]After
removing him, God made David their king. This is
what God said about him, 'I have found that David,
the son of Jesse, is the kind of man I like, a man who
will do all I want him to do.' [23]It was Jesus, a descendant of David, that God made the Saviour of the people of Israel, as he had promised. [24]Before Jesus began
his work, John preached to all the people of Israel that
they should turn from their sins and be baptized.
[25]And as John was about to finish his mission, he said
to the people, 'Who do you think I am? I am not the
one you are waiting for. But look! He is coming after
me, and I am not good enough to take his sandals off
his feet.'

[26]"My brothers, descendants of Abraham, and all
Gentiles here who worship God: it is to us that this
message of salvation has been sent! [27]For the people
who live in Jerusalem, and their leaders, did not know
that he is the Saviour, nor did they understand the
words of the prophets that are read every Sabbath day.
Yet they made the prophets' words come true by con-
demning Jesus. [28]And even though they could find no
reason to pass the death sentence on him, they asked
Pilate to have him put to death. [29]And after they had
done everything that the Scriptures say about him,
they took him down from the cross and placed him in
a grave. [30]But God raised him from the dead, [31]and for
many days he appeared to those who had travelled
with him from Galilee to Jerusalem. They are now
witnesses for him to the people of Israel. [32-33]And we
are here to bring the Good News to you: what God
promised our ancestors he would do, he has now done

for us, who are their descendants, by raising Jesus to
life. As it is written in the second Psalm,

> 'You are my Son;
>> today I have become your Father.'

³⁴And this is what God said about raising him from the
dead, never again to return to decay,

> 'I will give you the sacred and sure bless-
>> ings
> that I promised to David.'

³⁵As indeed he says in another passage,

> 'You will not allow your devoted servant
>> to suffer decay.'

³⁶For David served God's purposes in his own time;
and then he died, was buried beside his ancestors, and
suffered decay. ³⁷But the one whom God raised from
the dead did not suffer decay. ³⁸⁻³⁹All of you, my
brothers, are to know for sure that it is through Jesus
that the message about forgiveness of sins is preached
to you; you are to know that everyone who believes in
him is set free from all the sins from which the Law of
Moses could not set you free. ⁴⁰Take care, then, so
that what the prophets said may not happen to you,

⁴¹ 'Look, you scoffers! Wonder and die!
> For the work that I am doing in your
>> own day
> is something that you will not believe,
> even when someone explains it to
>> you!' "

⁴²As Paul and Barnabas were leaving the synagogue,
the people invited them to come back the next Sabbath
and tell them more about these things. ⁴³After the people had left the meeting, Paul and Barnabas were followed by many Jews and many Gentiles converted to
Judaism. The apostles spoke to them and encouraged
them to keep on living in the grace of God.

⁴⁴The next Sabbath day nearly everyone in the town
came to hear the word of the Lord. ⁴⁵When the Jews
saw the crowds, they were filled with jealousy; they
spoke against what Paul was saying and insulted him.
⁴⁶But Paul and Barnabas spoke out even more boldly,
"It was necessary that the word of God should be
spoken first to you. But since you reject it, and do not
consider yourselves worthy of eternal life, we will

leave you and go to the Gentiles. ⁴⁷For this is the
commandment that the Lord has given us,

'I have set you to be a light for the
        Gentiles,
    to be the way of salvation for the
        whole world.' "

⁴⁸When the Gentiles heard this they were glad and
praised the Lord's message; and those who had been
chosen for eternal life became believers.

Shook the dust off their feet against them

⁴⁹The word of the Lord spread everywhere in that
region. ⁵⁰But the Jews stirred up the leading men of
the city and the Gentile women of high social standing
who worshipped God. They started a persecution
against Paul and Barnabas, and threw them out of their
region. ⁵¹The apostles shook the dust off their feet
against them and went on to Iconium. ⁵²The disciples
in Antioch were full of joy and the Holy Spirit.

In Iconium

14 The same thing happened in Iconium: Paul and
    Barnabas went to the Jewish synagogue and

spoke in such a way that a great number of Jews and Gentiles became believers. ²But the Jews who would not believe stirred up the Gentiles and turned their feelings against the brothers. ³The apostles stayed there for a long time. They spoke boldly about the Lord, who proved that their message about his grace was true by giving them the power to perform miracles and wonders. ⁴The crowd in the city was divided: some were for the Jews, others for the apostles.

⁵Then the Gentiles and the Jews, together with their leaders, decided to mistreat the apostles and stone them. ⁶When the apostles learned about it they fled to Lystra and Derbe, cities in Lycaonia, and to the surrounding territory. ⁷There they preached the Good News.

In Lystra and Derbe

⁸There was a man living in Lystra whose feet were crippled; he had been lame from birth and had never been able to walk. ⁹Sitting there, he listened to Paul's words. Paul saw that he believed and could be healed, so he looked straight at him ¹⁰and said in a loud voice, "Stand up straight on your feet!" The man jumped up and started walking around.¹¹When the crowds saw what Paul had done, they started to shout in their own Lycaonian language, "The gods have become like men and have come down to us!" ¹²They gave Barnabas the name Zeus, and Paul the name Hermes, because he was the one who did the speaking. ¹³The priest of the god Zeus, whose temple stood just outside the town, brought bulls and flowers to the gate. He and the crowds wanted to offer sacrifice to the apostles.

¹⁴When Barnabas and Paul heard what they were about to do, they tore their clothes and ran into the middle of the crowd, shouting, ¹⁵"Why are you doing this, men? We are just men, human beings like you! We are here to announce the Good News, to turn you away from these worthless things to the living God, who made heaven, earth, sea, and all that is in them. ¹⁶In the past he allowed all peoples to go their own way. ¹⁷But he has always given proof of himself by the good things he does: he gives you rain from heaven and crops at the right times; he gives you food and fills your hearts with

And dragged him out of town

happiness." [18]Even with these words the apostles could hardly keep the crowds from offering a sacrifice to them.

[19]Some Jews came from Antioch of Pisidia and from Iconium; they won the crowds to their side, stoned Paul and dragged him out of town, thinking that he was dead. [20]But when the believers gathered round him, he got up and went back into the town. The next day he and Barnabas went to Derbe.

The Return to Antioch in Syria

[21]Paul and Barnabas preached the Good News in Derbe, and won many disciples. Then they went back to Lystra, then to Iconium, and then to Antioch of Pisidia. [22]They strengthened the believers and encouraged them to remain true to the faith. "We must pass through many troubles to enter the Kingdom of God," they taught. [23]In each church they appointed elders for them; and with prayers and fasting they commended them to the Lord, in whom they had put their trust.

[24]After going through the territory of Pisidia, they came to Pamphylia. [25]They preached the message in Perga and then went down to Attalia, [26]and from there they sailed back to Antioch, the place where they had been commended to the care of God's grace for the work they had now completed.

²⁷When they arrived in Antioch they gathered the people of the church together and told them of all that God had done with them, and how he had opened the way for the Gentiles to believe. ²⁸They stayed a long time there with the believers.

The Meeting at Jerusalem

15 Some men came from Judea to Antioch and started teaching the brothers, "You cannot be saved unless you are circumcised as the Law of Moses requires." ²Paul and Barnabas had a fierce argument and dispute with them about this; so it was decided that Paul and Barnabas and some of the others in Antioch should go to Jerusalem and see the apostles and elders about this matter.

³They were sent on their way by the church, and as they went through Phoenicia and Samaria they reported how the Gentiles had turned to God; this news brought great joy to all the brothers. ⁴When they arrived in Jerusalem, they were welcomed by the church, the apostles, and the elders, to whom they told all that God had done with them. ⁵But some of the believers who belonged to the party of the Pharisees stood up and said, "They have to be circumcised and told to obey the Law of Moses."

⁶The apostles and the elders met together to consider this question. ⁷After a long debate Peter stood up and said, "My brothers, you know that a long time ago God chose me from among you to preach the message of Good News to the Gentiles, so that they could hear and believe. ⁸And God, who knows the hearts of men, showed his approval of the Gentiles by giving the Holy Spirit to them, just as he had to us. ⁹He made no difference between us and them; he purified their hearts because they believed. ¹⁰So then, why do you want to put God to the test now by laying a load on the backs of the believers which neither our ancestors nor we ourselves were able to carry? ¹¹No! We believe and are saved by the grace of the Lord Jesus, just as they are."

¹²The whole group was silent as they heard Barnabas and Paul report all the wonders and miracles that God had done through them among the Gentiles. ¹³When

they finished speaking, James spoke up, "Listen to me, brothers! ¹⁴Simon has just explained how God first showed his care for the Gentiles by taking from among them a people to be all his own. ¹⁵The words of the prophets agree completely with this. As the scripture says,

¹⁶ 'After this I will return, says the Lord,
    and I will raise David's fallen house.
I will restore its ruins,
    and build it up again.
¹⁷ And so all other people will seek the Lord,
    all the Gentiles whom I have called to
    be my own.
¹⁸ So says the Lord, who made this known
    long ago.'

¹⁹"It is my opinion," James went on, "that we should not trouble the Gentiles who are turning to God. ²⁰Instead, we should write a letter telling them not to eat any food that is unclean because it has been offered to idols; to keep themselves from immorality; not to eat any animal that has been strangled, or any blood. ²¹For the Law of Moses has been read for a very long time in the synagogues every Sabbath, and his words are preached in every town."

The Letter to the Gentile Believers

²²Then the apostles and the elders, together with the whole church, decided to choose some men from the group and send them to Antioch with Paul and Barnabas. They chose Judas, called Barsabbas, and Silas, two men who were highly respected by the brothers. ²³They sent the following letter by them:

"We, the apostles and the elders, your brothers, send greetings to all brothers of Gentile birth who live in Antioch, Syria, and Cilicia. ²⁴We have heard that some men of our group went out and troubled and upset you by what they said; they had not, however, received any instructions from us to do this. ²⁵And so we have met together and have all agreed to choose some messengers and send them to you. They will go with our dear friends Barnabas and Paul, ²⁶who have risked their lives in the service of our Lord Jesus Christ. ²⁷We send you, then,

Judas and Silas, who will tell you in person the same
things we are writing. [28]The Holy Spirit and we have
agreed not to put any other burden on you besides these
necessary rules: [29]eat no food that has been offered to
idols; eat no blood; eat no animal that has been strangled; and keep yourselves from immorality. You will do
well if you keep yourselves from doing these things.
Good-bye."

[30]The messengers were sent off and went to Antioch,
where they gathered the whole group of believers and
gave them the letter. [31]When the people read the letter, they were filled with joy by the message of encouragement. [32]Judas and Silas, who were themselves
prophets, spoke a long time with the brothers, giving
them courage and strength. [33]After spending some
time there, they were sent off in peace by the brothers,
and went back to those who had sent them. [[34]But
Silas decided to stay there.]

[35]Paul and Barnabas spent some time in Antioch.
Together with many others, they taught and preached
the word of the Lord.

Paul and Barnabas Separate

[36]Some time later Paul said to Barnabas, "Let us go
back and visit our brothers in every city where we
preached the word of the Lord, and find out how they
are getting along." [37]Barnabas wanted to take John
Mark with them, [38]but Paul did not think it was right to
take him, because he had not stayed with them to the
end of their mission, but had turned back and left them
in Pamphylia. [39]They had a sharp argument between
them, and separated from each other. Barnabas took
Mark and sailed off for Cyprus, [40]while Paul chose Silas
and left, commended by the brothers to the care of the
Lord's grace. [41]He went through Syria and Cilicia,
strengthening the churches.

Timothy Goes with Paul and Silas

16 Paul travelled on to Derbe and Lystra. A believer
    named Timothy lived there; his mother, also a

believer, was Jewish, but his father was Greek. ²All the
brothers in Lystra and Iconium spoke well of Timothy.
³Paul wanted to take Timothy along with him, so he
circumcised him. He did so because all the Jews who
lived in those places knew that Timothy's father was
Greek. ⁴As they went through the towns they delivered
to the believers the rules decided upon by the apostles
and elders in Jerusalem, and told them to obey these
rules. ⁵So the churches were made stronger in the faith
and grew in numbers every day.

In Troas: Paul's Vision

⁶They travelled through the region of Phrygia and
Galatia, because the Holy Spirit did not let them preach
the message in the province of Asia. ⁷When they
reached the border of Mysia, they tried to go into the
province of Bithynia, but the Spirit of Jesus did not
allow them. ⁸So they travelled right on through Mysia
and went down to Troas. ⁹Paul had a vision that night
in which he saw a man of Macedonia standing and begging him, "Come over to Macedonia and help us!" ¹⁰As
soon as Paul had this vision, we got ready to leave for
Macedonia, because we decided that God had called us
to preach the Good News to the people there.

In Philippi: the Conversion of Lydia

¹¹We left by ship from Troas and sailed straight across
to Samothrace, and the next day to Neapolis. ¹²From
there we went inland to Philippi, a city of the first district of Macedonia; it is also a Roman colony. We spent
several days in that city. ¹³On the Sabbath day we went
out of the city to the riverside, where we thought there
would be a Jewish place for prayer. We sat down and
talked to the women who gathered there. ¹⁴One of those
who heard us was Lydia, from Thyatira, who was a
dealer in purple goods. She was a woman who worshipped God, and the Lord opened her mind to pay
attention to what Paul was saying. ¹⁵She and the people
of her house were baptized. Then she invited us, "Come
and stay in my house, if you have decided that I am a
true believer in the Lord." And she persuaded us to go.

In Prison at Philippi

¹⁶One day as we were going to the place of prayer, we were met by a slave girl who had an evil spirit in her that made her predict the future. She earned much money for her owners by telling fortunes. ¹⁷She followed Paul and us, shouting, "These men are servants of the Most High God! They announce to you how you can be saved!" ¹⁸She did this for many days, until Paul became so upset that he turned round and said to the spirit, "In the name of Jesus Christ I order you to come out of her!" The spirit went out of her that very moment. ¹⁹When her owners realized that their chance of making money was gone, they grabbed Paul and Silas and dragged them to the authorities in the public square. ²⁰They brought them before the Roman officials and said, "These men are Jews, and they are causing trouble in our city. ²¹They are teaching customs that are against our law; we are Romans and cannot accept or practise them." ²²The crowd joined the attack against them; the officials tore the clothes off Paul and Silas, and ordered them to be whipped. ²³After a severe beating they were thrown into jail, and the jailer was ordered to lock them up tight. ²⁴Upon receiving this order, the jailer threw them into the inner cell and fastened their feet between heavy blocks of wood.

²⁵About midnight Paul and Silas were praying and singing hymns to God, and the other prisoners were listening to them. ²⁶Suddenly there was a violent earthquake, which shook the prison to its foundations. At once all the doors opened, and the chains fell off all the prisoners. ²⁷The jailer woke up, and when he saw the prison doors open he thought that all the prisoners had escaped; so he pulled out his sword and was about to kill himself. ²⁸But Paul shouted at the top of his voice, "Don't harm yourself! We are all here!"

²⁹The jailer called for a light, rushed in, and fell trembling at the feet of Paul and Silas. ³⁰Then he led them out and asked, "What must I do, sirs, to be saved?"

³¹"Believe in the Lord Jesus," they said, "and you will be saved—you and your family." ³²Then they preached the word of the Lord to him and to all the

What must I do, sirs, to be saved?

others in his house. ³³At that very hour of the night the jailer took them and washed off their wounds; and he and all his family were baptized at once. ³⁴He took Paul and Silas up into his house and gave them some food to eat. He and his family were filled with joy, because he now believed in God.

³⁵The next morning the Roman authorities sent police officers with the order, "Let those men go."

³⁶So the jailer told it to Paul, "The officials have sent an order for you and Silas to be released. You may leave, then, and go in peace."

³⁷But Paul said to the police officers, "We were not found guilty of any crime, yet they whipped us in public—and we are Roman citizens! Then they threw us in prison. And now they want to send us away secretly? Not at all! The Roman officials themselves must come here and let us out."

³⁸The police officers reported these words to the Roman officials; and when they heard that Paul and Silas were Roman citizens, they were afraid. ³⁹So they went and apologized to them; then they led them out of the

prison and asked them to leave the city. ⁴⁰Paul and Silas left the prison and went to Lydia's house. There they met the brothers, spoke words of encouragement to them, and left.

In Thessalonica

17 They travelled on through Amphipolis and Apollonia, and came to Thessalonica, where there was a Jewish synagogue. ²According to his usual habit, Paul went to the synagogue. There during three Sabbath days he argued with the people from the Scriptures, ³explaining them and proving from them that the Messiah had to suffer, and rise from death. "This Jesus whom I announce to you," Paul said, "is the Messiah." ⁴Some of them were convinced and joined Paul and Silas; so did a large group of Greeks who worshipped God, and many of the leading women.

⁵But the Jews were jealous and gathered some of the worthless loafers from the streets and formed a mob. They set the whole city in an uproar, and attacked the home of Jason, trying to find Paul and Silas and bring them out to the people. ⁶But when they did not find them, they dragged Jason and some other brothers to the city authorities and shouted, "These men have caused trouble everywhere! Now they have come to our city, ⁷and Jason has kept them in his house. They are all breaking the laws of the Emperor, saying that there is another king, by the name of Jesus." ⁸With these words they threw the crowd and the city authorities in an uproar. ⁹The authorities made Jason and the others pay the required amount of money to be released, and then let them go.

In Berea

¹⁰As soon as night came, the brothers sent Paul and Silas to Berea. When they arrived, they went to the Jewish synagogue. ¹¹The people there were more open-minded than the people in Thessalonica. They listened to the message with great eagerness, and every day they studied the Scriptures to see if what Paul said was really true. ¹²Many of them believed; and many Greek women of high social standing and many Greek men also be-

lieved. [13]But when the Jews in Thessalonica heard that Paul had preached the word of God in Berea also, they came there and started exciting and stirring up the mobs. [14]At once the brothers sent Paul away to the coast; but both Silas and Timothy stayed in Berea. [15]The men who were taking Paul went with him as far as Athens. Then they went back to Berea with instructions from Paul that Silas and Timothy join him as soon as possible.

In Athens

[16]While Paul was waiting in Athens for Silas and Timothy, he was greatly upset when he noticed how full of idols the city was. [17]So he argued in the synagogue with the Jews and the Gentiles who worshipped God, and in the public square every day with the people who happened to come by. [18]Certain Epicurean and Stoic teachers also debated with him. Some said, "What is this ignorant show-off trying to say?"

Others said, "He seems to be talking about foreign gods." They said this because Paul was preaching about Jesus and the resurrection. [19]So they took Paul, brought him before the meeting of the Areopagus, and said, "We would like to know this new teaching that you are talking about. [20]Some of the things we hear you say sound strange to us, and we would like to know what they mean." [21](For all the citizens of Athens and the foreigners who lived there liked to spend all their time telling and hearing the latest new thing.)

[22]Paul stood up in front of the meeting of the Areopagus and said, "Men of Athens! I see that in every way you are very religious. [23]For as I walked through your city and looked at the places where you worship, I found also an altar on which is written, 'To an Unknown God.' That which you worship, then, even though you do not know it, is what I now proclaim to you. [24]God, who made the world and everything in it, is Lord of heaven and earth, and does not live in temples made by men. [25]Nor does he need anything that men can supply by working for him, since it is he himself who gives life and breath and everything else to all men. [26]From the one man he created all races of men, and made them live

over the whole earth. He himself fixed beforehand the
exact times and the limits of the places where they
would live. [27]He did this so that they would look for
him, and perhaps find him as they felt round for him.
Yet God is actually not far from any one of us; [28]as
someone has said,

> 'In him we live and move and exist.'

It is as some of your poets have said,

> 'We too are his children.'

[29]Since we are God's children, we should not suppose
that his nature is anything like an image of gold or silver
or stone, shaped by the art and skill of man. [30]God has
overlooked the times when men did not know, but now
he commands all men everywhere to turn away from
their evil ways. [31]For he has fixed a day in which he will
judge the whole world with justice, by means of a man
he has chosen. He has given proof of this to everyone
by raising that man from death!"

[32]When they heard Paul speak about a raising from
death, some of them made fun of him, but others said,
"We want to hear you speak about this again." [33]And
so Paul left the meeting. [34]Some men joined him and
believed; among them was Dionysius, a member of the
Areopagus, a woman named Damaris, and some
others.

In Corinth

18 After this, Paul left Athens and went on to Corinth. [2]There he met a Jew named Aquila, born in
Pontus, who had just come from Italy with his wife
Priscilla, because Emperor Claudius had ordered all the
Jews to leave Rome. Paul went to see them, [3]and stayed
and worked with them, because he earned his living by
making tents, just as they did. [4]He argued in the synagogue every Sabbath, trying to convince both Jews and
Greeks.

[5]When Silas and Timothy arrived from Macedonia,
Paul gave his whole time to preaching the message,
testifying to the Jews that Jesus is the Messiah. [6]When
they opposed him and said evil things about him, he
protested by shaking the dust from his clothes and saying to them, "If you are lost, you yourselves must take
the blame for it! I am not responsible. From now on I

He earned his living by making tents

will go to the Gentiles." ⁷So he left them and went to live in the house of a Gentile named Titius Justus, who worshipped God; his house was next to the synagogue. ⁸Crispus, the leader of the synagogue, believed in the Lord, he and all his family; and many other people in Corinth heard the message, believed, and were baptized.

⁹One night Paul had a vision, in which the Lord said to him, "Do not be afraid, but keep on speaking and do not give up, ¹⁰because I am with you. No one will be able to harm you, because many in this city are my people." ¹¹So Paul stayed there for a year and a half, teaching the people the word of God.

¹²When Gallio was made the Roman governor of Greece, the Jews got together, seized Paul and took him into court. ¹³"This man," they said, "is trying to persuade people to worship God in a way that is against the law!"

¹⁴Paul was about to speak, when Gallio said to the Jews, "If this were a matter of some wrong or evil crime that has been committed, it would be reasonable for me to be patient with you Jews. ¹⁵But since it is an argument about words and names and your own law, you yourselves must settle it. I will not be the judge of such things!" ¹⁶And he drove them out of the court.

¹⁷They all grabbed Sosthenes, the leader of the synagogue, and beat him in front of the court. But that did not bother Gallio a bit.

The Return to Antioch

¹⁸Paul stayed on in Corinth with the brothers for many days, then left them and sailed off with Priscilla and Aquila for Syria. Before sailing he made a vow in Cenchreae and had his head shaved. ¹⁹They arrived in Ephesus, where Paul left Priscilla and Aquila. He went into the synagogue and argued with the Jews. ²⁰They asked him to stay with them a long time, but he would not consent. ²¹Instead, he told them as he left, "If it is the will of God, I will come back to you." And so he sailed from Ephesus.
²²When he arrived at Caesarea he went to Jerusalem and greeted the church, and then went to Antioch. ²³After spending some time there he left. He went through the region of Galatia and Phrygia, strengthening all the believers.

Apollos in Ephesus and Corinth

²⁴A certain Jew named Apollos, born in Alexandria, came to Ephesus. He was an eloquent speaker and had a thorough knowledge of the Scriptures. ²⁵He had been instructed in the Way of the Lord, and with great enthusiasm spoke and taught correctly the facts about Jesus. However, he knew only the baptism of John. ²⁶He began to speak boldly in the synagogue. When Priscilla and Aquila heard him, they took him home with them and explained to him more correctly the Way of God. ²⁷Apollos decided to go to Greece, so the believers in Ephesus helped him by writing to their brothers in Greece, urging them to welcome him there. When he arrived, he was a great help to those who through God's grace had become believers. ²⁸For with his strong arguments he defeated the Jews in public debates, proving from the Scriptures that Jesus is the Messiah.

Paul in Ephesus

19 While Apollos was in Corinth, Paul travelled through the interior of the province and arrived

in Ephesus. There he found some disciples, ²and asked them, "Did you receive the Holy Spirit when you believed?"

"We have not even heard that there is a Holy Spirit," they answered.

³"Well, then, what kind of baptism did you receive?" Paul asked.

"The baptism of John," they answered.

⁴Paul said, "The baptism of John was for those who turned from their sins; and he told the people of Israel to believe in the one who was coming after him—that is, in Jesus."

⁵When they heard this, they were baptized in the name of the Lord Jesus. ⁶Paul placed his hands on them, and the Holy Spirit came upon them; they spoke in strange tongues and also proclaimed God's message. ⁷They were about twelve men in all.

⁸Paul went into the synagogue, and for three months spoke boldly with the people, arguing with them and trying to convince them about the Kingdom of God. ⁹But some of them were stubborn and would not believe, and said evil things about the Way of the Lord before the whole group. So Paul left them and took the disciples with him; and every day he held discussions in the lecture hall of Tyrannus. ¹⁰This went on for two years, so that all the people who lived in the province of Asia, both Jews and Gentiles, heard the word of the Lord.

The Sons of Sceva

¹¹God was performing unusual miracles through Paul. ¹²Even handkerchiefs and aprons he had used were taken to the sick, and their diseases were driven away and the evil spirits would go out of them. ¹³Some Jews who travelled round and drove out evil spirits also tried to use the name of the Lord Jesus to do this. They said to the evil spirits, "I command you in the name of Jesus, whom Paul preaches." ¹⁴There were seven sons of a Jewish High Priest named Sceva who were doing this.

¹⁵But the evil spirit said to them, "I know Jesus and I know about Paul; but you—who are you?"

¹⁶The man who had the evil spirit in him attacked them with such violence that he defeated them. They all

ran away from his house, wounded and with their clothes torn off. [17] All the Jews and Gentiles who lived in Ephesus heard about this; they were all filled with fear, and the name of the Lord Jesus was given greater honour. [18] Many of the believers came, publicly admitting and revealing what they had done. [19] Many of those who had practised magic brought their books together and burned them in the presence of everyone. They added up the price of the books and the total came to five thousand pounds. [20] In this powerful way the word of the Lord kept spreading and growing stronger.

The Riot in Ephesus

[21] After these things had happened, Paul made up his mind to travel through Macedonia and Greece and go on to Jerusalem. "After I go there," he said, "I must also see Rome." [22] So he sent Timothy and Erastus, two of his helpers, to Macedonia, while he spent more time in the province of Asia.

[23] It was at this time that there was serious trouble in Ephesus because of the Way of the Lord. [24] A certain silversmith named Demetrius made silver models of the temple of the goddess Artemis, and his business brought a great deal of profit to the workers. [25] So he called them all together, with others whose work was like theirs, and said to them, "Men, you know that our prosperity comes from this work. [26] You can see and hear for yourselves what this fellow Paul is doing. He says that gods made by men are not gods at all, and has succeeded in convincing many people, both here in Ephesus and in nearly the whole province of Asia. [27] There is the danger, then, that this business of ours will get a bad name. Not only that, there is also the danger that the temple of the great goddess Artemis will come to mean nothing, and that her greatness will be destroyed—the goddess worshipped by everyone in Asia and in all the world!"

[28] As the crowd heard these words they became furious, and started shouting, "Great is Artemis of Ephesus!" [29] The uproar spread throughout the whole city. The mob grabbed Gaius and Aristarchus, two Macedonians who were travelling with Paul, and rushed with them to the theatre. [30] Paul himself wanted to go before the crowd, but the believers would not let him.

³¹Some of the provincial authorities, who were his friends, also sent him a message begging him not to show himself in the theatre. ³²Meanwhile, the whole meeting was in an uproar: some people were shouting one thing, others were shouting something else, because most of them did not even know why they had come together. ³³Some of the people concluded that Alexander was responsible, since the Jews made him go up to the front. Then Alexander motioned with his hand and tried to make a speech of defence before the people. ³⁴But when they recognized that he was a Jew, they all shouted together the same thing for two hours, "Great is Artemis of Ephesus!"

³⁵At last the city clerk was able to calm the crowd. "Men of Ephesus!" he said. "Everyone knows that the city of Ephesus is the keeper of the temple of the great Artemis and of the sacred stone that fell down from heaven. ³⁶Nobody can deny these things. So then, you must calm down and not do anything reckless. ³⁷You have brought these men here, even though they have not robbed temples or said evil things about our goddess. ³⁸If Demetrius and his workers have an accusation against someone, there are the regular days for court and there are the authorities; they can accuse each other there. ³⁹But if there is something more that you want, it will have to be settled in the legal meeting of citizens. ⁴⁰For there is the danger that we will be accused of a riot in what has happened today. There is no excuse for all this uproar, and we would not be able to give a good reason for it." ⁴¹After saying this, he dismissed the meeting.

To Macedonia and Greece

20 After the uproar died down, Paul called together the believers, and with words of encouragement said good-bye to them. Then he left and went on to Macedonia. ²He went through those regions and encouraged the people with many messages. Then he came to Greece, ³where he stayed three months. He was getting ready to go to Syria when he discovered that the Jews were plotting against him; so he decided to go back through Macedonia. ⁴Sopater, the son of Pyrrhus, from

Berea, went with him; so did Aristarchus and Secundus, from Thessalonica; Gaius, from Derbe; Timothy; and Tychicus and Trophimus, from the province of Asia. ⁵They went ahead and waited for us in Troas. ⁶We sailed from Philippi after the Feast of Unleavened Bread, and five days later joined them in Troas, where we spent a week.

Eutychus got sleepier and sleepier

Paul's Last Visit in Troas

⁷On Saturday evening we gathered together for the fellowship meal. Paul spoke to the people, and kept on speaking until midnight, since he was going to leave the next day. ⁸There were many lamps in the upstairs room where we were meeting. ⁹A young man named Eutychus was sitting in the window; and as Paul kept on talking, Eutychus got sleepier and sleepier, until he finally went sound asleep and fell from the third story to the ground. They picked him up, and he was dead.

¹⁰But Paul went down and threw himself on him and hugged him. "Don't worry," he said, "he is still alive!" ¹¹Then he went back upstairs, broke bread, and ate. After talking with them for a long time until sunrise, Paul left. ¹²They took the young man home alive, and were greatly comforted.

From Troas to Miletus

¹³We went on ahead to the ship and sailed off to Assos, where we were going to take Paul aboard. He had told us to do this, because he was going there by land. ¹⁴When he met us in Assos, we took him aboard and went on to Mitylene. ¹⁵We sailed from there and arrived off Chios the next day. A day later we came to Samos, and the following day we reached Miletus. ¹⁶Paul had decided to sail on by Ephesus, so as not to lose any time in the province of Asia. He was in a hurry to arrive in Jerusalem, if at all possible, by the day of Pentecost.

Paul's Farewell Speech to the Elders of Ephesus

¹⁷Paul sent a message from Miletus to Ephesus, asking the elders of the church to meet him. ¹⁸When they arrived he said to them, "You know how I spent the whole time I was with you, from the first day I arrived in the province of Asia. ¹⁹With all humility and many tears I did my work as the Lord's servant, through the hard times that came to me because of the plots of the Jews. ²⁰You know that I did not hold back anything that would be of help to you as I preached and taught you in public and in your homes. ²¹To Jews and Gentiles alike I gave solemn warning that they should turn from their sins to God, and believe in our Lord Jesus. ²²And now, in obedience to the Holy Spirit, I am going to Jerusalem, not knowing what will happen to me there. ²³I only know that in every city the Holy Spirit has warned me that prison and troubles wait for me. ²⁴But I reckon my own life to be worth nothing to me, in order that I may complete my mission and finish the work that the Lord Jesus gave me to do, which is to declare the Good News of the grace of God.

²⁵"I have gone about among all of you, preaching the Kingdom of God. And now I know that none of you will

ever see me again. ²⁶So I solemnly declare to you this very day: if any of you should be lost, I am not responsible. ²⁷For I have not held back from announcing to you the whole purpose of God. ²⁸Keep watch over yourselves and over all the flock which the Holy Spirit has placed in your care. Be shepherds of the church of God, which he made his own through the death of his own Son. ²⁹I know that after I leave, fierce wolves will come among you, and they will not spare the flock. ³⁰The time will come when some men from your own group will tell lies to lead the believers away after them. ³¹Watch, then, and remember that with many tears, day and night, I taught every one of you for three years.

³²"And now I place you in the care of God and the message of his grace. He is able to build you up and give you the blessings he keeps for all his people. ³³I have not coveted anyone's silver or gold or clothing. ³⁴You yourselves know that with these hands of mine I have worked and provided everything that my companions and I have needed. ³⁵I have shown you in all things that by working hard in this way we must help the weak, remembering the words that the Lord Jesus himself said, 'There is more happiness in giving than in receiving.' "

³⁶When Paul finished, he knelt down with them all and prayed. ³⁷They were all crying as they hugged him and kissed him good-bye. ³⁸They were especially sad at the words he had said that they would never see him again. And so they went with him to the ship.

Paul Goes to Jerusalem

21 We said good-bye to them and left. After sailing straight across, we came to Cos; the next day we reached Rhodes, and from there we went on to Patara. ²There we found a ship that was going to Phoenicia; so we went aboard and sailed away. ³We came to where we could see Cyprus, and sailed south of it on to Syria. We went ashore at Tyre, where the ship was going to unload its cargo. ⁴We found some believers there, and stayed with them a week. By the power of the Spirit they told Paul not to go to Jerusalem. ⁵But when our time with them was over, we left and went on our way. All of

Knelt down on the beach and prayed

them, with their wives and children, went with us out of the city. We all knelt down on the beach and prayed. ⁶Then we said good-bye to one another, and we went on board the ship while they went back home.

⁷We continued our voyage, sailing from Tyre to Ptolemais, where we greeted the brothers and stayed with them for a day. ⁸On the following day we left and arrived in Caesarea. There we went to the house of the evangelist Philip, and stayed with him. He was one of the seven men who had been chosen in Jerusalem. ⁹He had four unmarried daughters who proclaimed God's message. ¹⁰We had been there for several days when a prophet named Agabus arrived from Judea. ¹¹He came to us, took Paul's belt, tied up his own feet and hands with it, and said, "This is what the Holy Spirit says: The owner of this belt will be tied up in this way by the Jews in Jerusalem, and they will hand him over to the Gentiles."

¹²When we heard this, we and the others there begged Paul not to go to Jerusalem. ¹³But he answered, "What are you doing, crying like this and breaking my heart? I am ready not only to be tied up in Jerusalem but even to die there for the sake of the Lord Jesus."

¹⁴We could not convince him, so we gave up and said, "May the Lord's will be done."

¹⁵After spending some time there, we got our things ready and left for Jerusalem. ¹⁶Some of the disciples from Caesarea also went with us, and took us to the house of the man we were going to stay with—Mna-

son, from Cyprus, who had been a believer since the early days.

Paul Visits James

[17]When we arrived in Jerusalem the brothers welcomed us warmly. [18]The next day Paul went with us to see James; and all the church elders were present. [19]Paul greeted them and gave a complete report of everything that God had done among the Gentiles through his work. [20]After hearing him, they all praised God. Then they said to Paul, "You can see how it is, brother. There are thousands of Jews who have become believers, and they are all very devoted to the Law. [21]They have been told about you that you have been teaching all the Jews who live in Gentile countries to abandon the Law of Moses, telling them not to circumcise their children or follow the Jewish customs. [22]They are sure to hear that you have arrived. What should be done, then? [23]Do what we tell you. There are four men here who have taken a vow. [24]Go along with them and join them in the ceremony of purification and pay their expenses; then they will be able to shave their heads. In this way everyone will know that there is no truth in any of the things that they have been told about you, but that you yourself live in accordance with the Law of Moses. [25]But as to the Gentiles who have become believers, we have sent them a letter telling them we decided that they must not eat any food that has been offered to idols, or any blood, or any animal that has been strangled, and that they must keep themselves from immorality."

[26]So Paul took the men and the next day performed the ceremony of purification with them. Then he went into the temple and gave notice of how many days it would be until the end of the period of purification, when the sacrifice for each one of them would be offered.

Paul Arrested in the Temple

[27]When the seven days were about to come to an end, some Jews from the province of Asia saw Paul in the temple. They stirred up the whole crowd and grabbed

Paul. 28"Men of Israel!" they shouted. "Help! This is the man who goes everywhere teaching everyone against the people of Israel, the Law of Moses, and this temple. And now he has even brought some Gentiles into the temple and defiled this holy place!" 29(They said this because they had seen Trophimus from Ephesus with Paul in the city, and they thought that Paul had taken him into the temple.)

The mob was trying to kill Paul

30Confusion spread through the whole city, and the people all ran together, grabbed Paul, and dragged him out of the temple. At once the temple doors were closed. 31The mob was trying to kill Paul when a report was sent up to the commander of the Roman troops that all of Jerusalem was rioting. 32At once the commander took some officers and soldiers and rushed down to the crowd. When the people saw him with the soldiers, they stopped beating Paul. 33The commander went over to Paul, arrested him, and ordered him to be tied up with two chains. Then he asked, "Who is this man, and what has he done?" 34Some in the crowd shouted one thing, others something else. There was such confusion that the commander could not find out exactly what had happened; so he ordered his men to take Paul up into the fort. 35They got with him to the steps, and then the soldiers had to carry him because the mob was so wild. 36They were all coming after him and screaming, "Kill him!"

Paul Defends Himself

³⁷As they were about to take Paul into the fort, he spoke to the commander, "May I say something to you?"

"Do you speak Greek?" the commander asked. ³⁸"Then you are not that Egyptian fellow who some time ago started a revolution and led four thousand armed terrorists out into the desert?"

³⁹Paul answered, "I am a Jew, born in Tarsus of Cilicia, a citizen of an important city. Please, let me speak to the people."

⁴⁰The commander gave him permission, so Paul stood on the steps and motioned with his hand to the people. When they were quiet, Paul spoke to them in Hebrew,

22 "Men, brothers and fathers, listen to me as I make my defence before you!" ²When they heard him speaking to them in Hebrew, they were even quieter; and Paul went on,

³"I am a Jew, born in Tarsus of Cilicia, but brought up here in Jerusalem as a student of Gamaliel. I received strict instruction in the Law of our ancestors, and was just as dedicated to God as all of you here today are. ⁴I persecuted to the death the people who followed this Way. I arrested men and women and threw them into prison. ⁵The High Priest and the whole Council can prove that I am telling the truth. I received from them letters written to the Jewish brothers in Damascus, so I went there to arrest these people and bring them back in chains to Jerusalem to be punished."

Paul Tells of His Conversion
(Also Acts 9.1–19; 26.12–18)

⁶"As I was travelling and coming near Damascus, about midday a bright light from the sky flashed suddenly round me. ⁷I fell to the ground and heard a voice saying to me, 'Saul, Saul! Why do you persecute me?' ⁸'Who are you, Lord?' I asked. 'I am Jesus of Nazareth, whom you persecute,' he said to me. ⁹The men with me saw the light but did not hear the voice of the one who was speaking to me. ¹⁰I asked, 'What shall I do, Lord?' and the Lord said to me, 'Get up and go into Damascus,

and there you will be told everything that God has determined for you to do.' ¹¹I was blind because of the bright light, and so my companions took me by the hand and led me into Damascus.

¹²"There was a man named Ananias, a religious man who obeyed our Law and was highly respected by all the Jews living in Damascus. ¹³He came to me, stood by me and said, 'Brother Saul, see again!' At that very moment I saw again and looked at him. ¹⁴He said, 'The God of our ancestors has chosen you to know his will, to see his righteous Servant, and hear him speaking with his own voice. ¹⁵For you will be a witness for him to tell all men what you have seen and heard. ¹⁶And now, why wait any longer? Get up and be baptized and have your sins washed away by calling on his name.' "

Paul's Call to Preach to the Gentiles

¹⁷"I went back to Jerusalem, and while I was praying in the temple I had a vision, ¹⁸in which I saw the Lord as he said to me, 'Hurry and leave Jerusalem quickly, because the people here will not accept your witness about me.' ¹⁹'Lord,' I answered, 'they know very well that I went to the synagogues and arrested and beat those who believe in you. ²⁰And when your witness Stephen was put to death, I myself was there, approving of his murder and taking care of the cloaks of his murderers.' ²¹'Go,' the Lord said to me, 'because I will send you far away to the Gentiles.' "

²²The people listened to Paul until he said this; but then they started shouting at the top of their voices, "Away with him! Kill him! He's not fit to live!"²³They were screaming, waving their clothes, and throwing dust up in the air. ²⁴The Roman commander ordered his men to take Paul into the fort, and told them to whip him to find out why the Jews were screaming like this against him. ²⁵But when they had tied him up to be whipped, Paul said to the officer standing there, "Is it lawful for you to whip a Roman citizen who hasn't even been tried for any crime?"

²⁶When the officer heard this, he went to the commander and asked him, "What are you doing? That man is a Roman citizen!"

²⁷So the commander went to Paul and asked him, "Tell me, are you a Roman citizen?"

"Yes," answered Paul.

²⁸The commander said, "I became one by paying a large amount of money."

"But I am one by birth," Paul answered.

²⁹At once the men who were going to question Paul drew back from him; and the commander was afraid when he realized that Paul was a Roman citizen, and that he had put him in chains.

Paul before the Council

³⁰The commander wanted to find out for sure what the Jews were accusing Paul of; so the next day he had Paul's chains taken off and ordered the chief priests and the whole Council to meet. Then he took Paul, and made him stand before them.

23 Paul looked straight at the Council and said, "My brothers! My conscience is perfectly clear about my whole life before God, to this very day." ²The High Priest Ananias ordered those who were standing close to Paul to strike him on the mouth. ³Paul said to him, "God will certainly strike you—you whitewashed wall! You sit there to judge me according to the Law, yet you break the Law by ordering them to strike me!"

⁴The men close to Paul said to him, "You are insulting God's High Priest!"

⁵Paul answered, "I did not know, my brothers, that he was the High Priest. The scripture says, 'You must not speak evil of the ruler of your people.'"

⁶When Paul saw that some of the group were Sadducees and that others were Pharisees, he called out in the Council, "My brothers! I am a Pharisee, the son of Pharisees. I am on trial here because I hope that the dead will rise to life!" ⁷As soon as he said this, the Pharisees and Sadducees started to quarrel, and the group was divided. ⁸(For the Sadducees say that people will not rise from death, and that there are no angels or spirits; but the Pharisees believe in all three.) ⁹The shouting became louder, and some of the teachers of the Law who belonged to the party of the Pharisees stood up and protested strongly, "We cannot find a thing

wrong with this man! Perhaps a spirit or an angel really did speak to him!"

¹⁰The argument became so violent that the commander was afraid that Paul would be torn to pieces by them. So he ordered his soldiers to go down into the group and get Paul away from them, and take him into the fort.

¹¹The following night the Lord stood by Paul and said, "Courage! You have given your witness to me here in Jerusalem, and you must do the same in Rome also."

The Plot against Paul's Life

¹²The next morning some Jews met together and made a plan. They took a vow that they would not eat or drink anything until they had killed Paul. ¹³There were more than forty of them who planned this together. ¹⁴Then they went to the chief priests and elders and said, "We have taken a solemn vow together not to eat a thing until we kill Paul. ¹⁵Now then, you and the Council send word to the Roman commander to bring Paul down to you, pretending that you want to get more accurate information about him. But we will be ready to kill him before he ever gets here."

¹⁶But the son of Paul's sister heard of the plot; so he went and entered the fort and told it to Paul. ¹⁷Then Paul called one of the officers and said to him, "Take this young man to the commander; he has something to tell him." ¹⁸The officer took him, led him to the commander and said, "The prisoner Paul called me and asked me to bring this young man to you, because he has something to say to you."

¹⁹The commander took him by the hand, led him off by himself and asked him, "What do you have to tell me?"

²⁰He said, "The Jewish authorities have agreed to ask you tomorrow to take Paul down to the Council, pretending that the Council wants to get more accurate information about him. ²¹But don't listen to them, because there are more than forty men who will be hiding and waiting for him. They have taken a vow not to eat or drink until they kill him. They are now ready to do it, and are waiting for your decision."

²²The commander said, "Don't tell anyone that you have reported this to me." And he sent the young man away.

Paul Sent to Governor Felix

²³Then the commander called two of his officers and said, "Get two hundred soldiers ready to go to Caesarea, together with seventy horsemen and two hundred spearmen, and be ready to leave by nine o'clock tonight. ²⁴Provide some horses for Paul to ride, and get him safely through to Governor Felix." ²⁵Then the commander wrote a letter that went like this:
²⁶"Claudius Lysias to his Excellency, the Governor Felix: Greetings. ²⁷The Jews seized this man and were about to kill him. I learned that he is a Roman citizen, so I went with my soldiers and rescued him. ²⁸I wanted to know what they were accusing him of, so I took him down to their Council. ²⁹I found out that he had not done a thing for which he deserved to die or be put in prison; the accusation against him had to do with questions about their own law. ³⁰And when I was informed that some Jews were making a plot against him, I decided to send him to you. I told his accusers to make their charges against him before you."
³¹The soldiers carried out their orders. They got Paul and took him that night as far as Antipatris. ³²The next day the foot soldiers returned to the fort and left the horsemen to go on with him. ³³They took him to Caesarea, delivered the letter to the Governor, and turned Paul over to him. ³⁴The Governor read the letter and asked Paul what province he was from. When he found out that he was from Cilicia, ³⁵he said, "I will hear you when your accusers arrive." Then he gave orders that Paul be kept under guard in Herod's palace.

Paul Accused by the Jews

24 Five days later the High Priest Ananias went to Caesarea with some elders and a lawyer named Tertullus. They appeared before Governor Felix and made their charges against Paul. ²Tertullus was called and began to accuse Paul as follows:
"Your Excellency! Your wise leadership has brought

us a long period of peace, and many necessary reforms are being made for the good of our country. [3]We welcome this everywhere at all times, and we are deeply grateful to you. [4]I do not want to take up too much of your time, however, so I beg you to be kind and listen to our brief account. [5]We found this man to be a dangerous nuisance; he starts riots among the Jews all over the world, and is a leader of the party of the Nazarenes. [6]He also tried to defile the temple, and we arrested him. [We planned to judge him according to our own Law, [7]but the commander Lysias came in and with great violence took him from us. [8]Then Lysias gave orders that his accusers should come before you.] If you question this man, you yourself will be able to learn from him all the things that we are accusing him of." [9]The Jews joined in the accusation and said that all this was true.

Paul's Defence before Felix

[10]The Governor then motioned to Paul to speak, and Paul said,

"I know that you have been a judge over this nation for many years, and so I am happy to defend myself before you. [11]As you can find out for yourself, it was no more than twelve days ago that I went up to Jerusalem to worship. [12]The Jews did not find me arguing with anyone in the temple, nor did they find me stirring up the people, either in the synagogues or anywhere else in the city. [13]Nor can they give you proof of the accusations they now bring against me. [14]I do admit this to you: I worship the God of our ancestors by following that Way which they say is false. But I also believe in all the things written in the Law of Moses and the books of the prophets. [15]I have the same hope in God that these themselves hold, that all men, both the good and the bad, will rise from death. [16]And so I do my best always to have a clear conscience before God and men.

[17]"After being away from Jerusalem for several years, I went there to take some money to my own people and to offer sacrifices. [18]It was while I was doing this that they found me in the temple, after I had completed the ceremony of purification. There was no crowd with me, and no disorder. [19]But some Jews from the province of

Asia were there; they themselves ought to come before you and make their accusations, if they have anything against me. [20]Or let these men here tell what crime they found me guilty of when I stood before the Council— [21]except for the one thing I called out when I stood before them: 'I am being judged by you today for believing that the dead will rise to life.'"

[22]Then Felix, who was well informed about the Way, brought the hearing to a close. "I will decide your case," he told them, "when the commander Lysias arrives." [23]He ordered the officer in charge of Paul to keep him under guard, but to give him some freedom and allow his friends to provide for his needs.

Paul before Felix and Drusilla

[24]After some days Felix came with his wife Drusilla, who was Jewish. He sent for Paul and listened to him as he talked about faith in Christ Jesus. [25]But as Paul went on discussing about goodness, self-control, and the coming Day of Judgment, Felix was afraid and said, "You may leave now. I will call you again when I get the chance." [26]At the same time he was hoping that Paul would give him some money; and for this reason he would call for him often and talk with him.

[27]After two years had passed, Porcius Festus took the place of Felix as governor. Felix wanted to gain favour with the Jews, so he left Paul in prison.

Paul Appeals to the Emperor

25 Three days after Festus arrived in the province, he went from Caesarea to Jerusalem. [2]There the chief priests and the Jewish leaders brought their charges against Paul. They begged Festus [3]to do them the favour of having Paul come to Jerusalem, because they had made a plot to kill him on the way. [4]Festus answered, "Paul is being kept a prisoner in Caesarea, and I myself will be going back there soon. [5]Let your leaders go to Caesarea with me and accuse the man, if he has done anything wrong."

[6]Festus spent another eight or ten days with them, and then went to Caesarea. On the next day he sat down in the judgment court, and ordered Paul to be brought

in. ⁷When Paul arrived, the Jews who had come from Jerusalem stood round him and started making many serious charges against him, which they were not able to prove. ⁸But Paul defended himself, "I have done nothing wrong against the Law of the Jews, or the temple, or the Roman Emperor."

⁹Festus wanted to gain favour with the Jews, so he asked Paul, "Would you be willing to go to Jerusalem and be tried on these charges before me there?"

¹⁰Paul said, "I am standing before the Emperor's own judgment court, where I should be tried. I have done no wrong to the Jews, as you yourself well know. ¹¹If I have broken the law and done something for which I deserve the death penalty, I do not ask to escape it. But if there is no truth in the charges they bring against me, no one can hand me over to them. I appeal to the Emperor."

¹²Then Festus, after conferring with his advisers, answered, "You have appealed to the Emperor, so to the Emperor you will go."

Paul before Agrippa and Bernice

¹³Some time later King Agrippa and Bernice came to Caesarea to pay a visit of welcome to Festus. ¹⁴After they had been there several days, Festus explained Paul's situation to the king, "There is a man here who was left a prisoner by Felix; ¹⁵and when I went to Jerusalem, the Jewish chief priests and elders brought charges against him and asked me to condemn him. ¹⁶But I told them that the Romans are not in the habit of handing over any man accused of a crime before he has met his accusers face to face, and has the chance of defending himself against the accusation. ¹⁷When they came here, then, I lost no time, but on the very next day I sat in the judgment court and ordered the man to be brought in. ¹⁸His opponents stood up, but they did not accuse him of any of the evil crimes that I thought they would. ¹⁹All they had were some arguments with him about their own religion and about a man named Jesus, who has died; but Paul claims that he is alive. ²⁰I was undecided about how I could get information on these matters, so I asked Paul if he would be willing to go to Jerusalem

and be tried there on these charges. ²¹But Paul appealed; he asked to be kept under guard and let the Emperor decide his case. So I gave orders for him to be kept under guard until I could send him to the Emperor."

²²Agrippa said to Festus, "I would like to hear this man myself."

"You will hear him tomorrow," Festus answered.

²³The next day Agrippa and Bernice came with great pomp and ceremony, and entered the audience hall with the military chiefs and the leading men of the city. Festus gave the order and Paul was brought in. ²⁴Festus said, "King Agrippa, and all who are here with us: You see this man against whom all the Jewish people, both here and in Jerusalem, have brought complaints to me. They scream that he should not live any longer. ²⁵But I could not find that he had done anything for which he deserved the death sentence. And since he himself made an appeal to the Emperor, I have decided to send him. ²⁶But I do not have anything definite about him to write to the Emperor. So I have brought him here before you—and especially before you, King Agrippa!—so that, after investigating his case, I may have something to write. ²⁷For it seems unreasonable to me to send a prisoner without clearly indicating the charges against him."

Paul Defends Himself before Agrippa

26 Agrippa said to Paul, "You have permission to speak on your own behalf." Paul stretched out his hand and defended himself as follows:

²"King Agrippa! I consider myself fortunate that today I am to defend myself before you from all the things the Jews accuse me of. ³This is especially true because you know so well all the Jewish customs and questions. I ask you, then, to listen to me with patience.

⁴"All the Jews know how I have lived ever since I was young. They know from the beginning how I have spent my whole life in my own country and in Jerusalem. ⁵They have always known, if they are willing to testify, that from the very first I have lived as a member of the strictest party of our religion, the Pharisees. ⁶And now I stand here to be tried because I hope in the promise that God made to our ancestors—⁷the very promise that

all twelve tribes of our people hope to receive, as they worship God day and night. And it is because of this hope, your Majesty, that I am being accused by the Jews! ⁸Why do you Jews find it impossible to believe that God raises the dead?

⁹"I myself thought that I should do everything I could against the name of Jesus of Nazareth. ¹⁰That is what I did in Jerusalem. I received authority from the chief priests and put many of God's people in prison; and when they were sentenced to death, I also voted for it. ¹¹Many times I had them punished in all the synagogues, and tried to make them deny their faith. I was so furious with them that I even went to foreign cities to persecute them."

Paul Tells of His Conversion
(Also Acts 9.1–19; 22.6–16)

¹²"It was for this purpose that I went to Damascus with the authority and orders from the chief priests. ¹³It was on the road at midday, your Majesty, that I saw a light much brighter than the sun shining from the sky round me and the men travelling with me. ¹⁴All of us fell to the ground, and I heard a voice say to me in the Hebrew language, 'Saul, Saul! Why are you persecuting me? You hurt yourself by hitting back, like an ox kicking against its owner's stick.' ¹⁵'Who are you, Lord?' I asked. And the Lord said: 'I am Jesus, whom you persecute. ¹⁶But get up and stand on your feet. I have appeared to you to appoint you as my servant; you are to tell others what you have seen of me today, and what I will show you in the future. ¹⁷I will save you from the people of Israel and from the Gentiles, to whom I will send you. ¹⁸You are to open their eyes and turn them from the darkness to the light, and from the power of Satan to God, so that through their faith in me they will have their sins forgiven and receive their place among God's chosen people.' "

Paul Tells of His Work

¹⁹"And so, King Agrippa, I did not disobey the vision I had from heaven. ²⁰First in Damascus and in Jerusalem, and then in the whole country of the Jews and among the Gentiles, I preached that they must repent of

their sins and turn to God, and do the things that would show they had repented. [21]It was for this reason that the Jews seized me while I was in the temple, and tried to kill me. [22]But to this very day I have been helped by God, and so I stand here giving my witness to all, to the small and great alike. What I say is the very same thing the prophets and Moses said was going to happen: [23]that the Messiah must suffer and be the first one to rise from death, to announce the light of salvation to the Jews and to the Gentiles."

[24]As Paul defended himself in this way, Festus shouted at him, "You are mad, Paul! Your great learning is driving you mad!"

[25]Paul answered, "I am not mad, your Excellency! The words I speak are true and sober. [26]King Agrippa! I can speak to you with all boldness, because you know about these things. I am sure that you have taken notice of every one of them, for this thing has not happened hidden away in a corner. [27]King Agrippa, do you believe the prophets? I know that you do!"

[28]Agrippa said to Paul, "In this short time do you think you will make me a Christian?"

[29]"Whether a short time or a long time," Paul answered, "my prayer to God is that you and all the rest of you who are listening to me today might become what I am—except, of course, for these chains!"

[30]Then the king, the governor, Bernice, and all the others got up, [31]and after leaving they said to each other, "This man has not done anything for which he should die or be put in prison." [32]And Agrippa said to Festus, "This man could have been released if he had not appealed to the Emperor."

Paul Sails for Rome

27 When it was decided that we should sail to Italy, they handed Paul and some other prisoners over to Julius, an officer in the Roman army regiment called "The Emperor's Regiment." [2]We went aboard a ship from Adramyttium, which was ready to leave for the seaports of the province of Asia, and sailed away. Aristarchus, a Macedonian from Thessalonica, was with us. [3]The next day we arrived at Sidon. Julius was kind to Paul and allowed him to go and see his friends, to be

given what he needed. ⁴We went on from there, and because the winds were blowing against us we sailed on the sheltered side of the island of Cyprus. ⁵We crossed over the sea off Cilicia and Pamphylia, and came to Myra, in Lycia. ⁶There the officer found a ship from Alexandria that was going to sail for Italy, so he put us aboard.

⁷We sailed slowly for several days, and with great difficulty finally arrived off the town of Cnidus. The wind would not let us go any farther in that direction, so we sailed down the sheltered side of the island of Crete, passing by Cape Salmone. ⁸We kept close to the coast, and with great difficulty came to a place called Safe Harbours, not far from the town of Lasea.

⁹We spent a long time there, until it became dangerous to continue the voyage, because by now the day of Atonement was already past. So Paul gave them this advice, ¹⁰"Men, I see that our voyage from here on will be dangerous; there will be great damage to the cargo and to the ship, and loss of life as well." ¹¹But the army officer was convinced by what the captain and the owner of the ship said, and not by what Paul said. ¹²The harbour was not a good one to spend the winter in; so most of the men were in favour of putting out to sea and trying to reach Phoenix, if possible. It is a harbour in Crete that faces southwest and northwest, and they could spend the winter there.

The Storm at Sea

¹³A soft wind from the south began to blow, and the men thought that they could carry out their plan; so they pulled up the anchor and sailed as close as possible along the coast of Crete. ¹⁴But soon a very strong wind—the one called "Northeaster"—blew down from the island. ¹⁵It hit the ship, and since it was impossible to keep the ship headed into the wind, we gave up trying and let it be carried along by the wind. ¹⁶We got some shelter when we passed to the south of the little island of Cauda. There, with some difficulty, we managed to make the ship's boat secure. ¹⁷They pulled it aboard, and then fastened some ropes tight round the ship. They were afraid that they might run into the sandbanks off the

coast of Libya; so they lowered the sail and let the ship be carried by the wind. [18]The violent storm continued, so on the next day they began to throw the ship's cargo overboard, [19]and on the following day they threw the ship's equipment overboard with their own hands. [20]For many days we could not see the sun or the stars, and the wind kept on blowing very hard. We finally gave up all hope of being saved.

[21]After the men had gone a long time without food, Paul stood before them and said, "Men, you should have listened to me and not have sailed from Crete; then we would have avoided all this damage and loss. [22]But now I beg you, take courage! Not one of you will lose his life; only the ship will be lost. [23]For last night an angel of the God to whom I belong and whom I worship came to me [24]and said, 'Don't be afraid, Paul! You must stand before the Emperor; and God, in his goodness, has given you the lives of all those who are sailing with you.' [25]And so, men, take courage! For I trust in God that it will be just as I was told. [26]But we will be driven ashore on some island."

[27]It was the fourteenth night, and we were being driven by the storm on the Mediterranean. About midnight the sailors suspected that we were getting close to land. [28]So they dropped a line with a weight tied to it and found that the water was one hundred and twenty feet deep; a little later they did the same and found that it was ninety feet deep. [29]They were afraid that our ship would go on the rocks, so they lowered four anchors from the back of the ship and prayed for daylight. [30]The sailors tried to escape from the ship; they lowered the boat into the water and pretended that they were going to put out some anchors from the front of the ship. [31]But Paul said to the army officer and soldiers, "If these sailors don't stay on board, you cannot be saved." [32]So the soldiers cut the ropes that held the boat and let it go.

[33]Day was about to come, and Paul begged them all to eat some food, "You have been waiting for fourteen days now, and all this time you have not eaten a thing. [34]I beg you, then, eat some food; you need it in order to survive. Not even a hair of your heads will be lost." [35]After saying this, Paul took some bread, gave thanks

to God before them all, broke it, and began to eat. [36]They took courage, and every one of them also ate some food. [37]There was a total of two hundred and seventy-six of us on board. [38]After everyone had eaten enough, they lightened the ship by throwing the wheat into the sea.

The Shipwreck

[39]When day came, the sailors did not recognize the coast, but they noticed a bay with a beach and decided that, if possible, they would run the ship aground there. [40]So they cut off the anchors and let them sink in the sea, and at the same time they untied the ropes that held the steering oars. Then they raised the sail at the front of the ship so that the wind would blow the ship forward, and headed for shore. [41]But the ship hit a sandbank and went aground; the front part of the ship got stuck and could not move, while the back part was being broken to pieces by the violence of the waves.

Holding on to the planks

[42]The soldiers made a plan to kill all the prisoners, so that none of them would swim ashore and escape. [43]But the army officer wanted to save Paul, so he stopped them from doing this. Instead, he ordered all the men who could swim to jump overboard first and swim ashore; [44]the rest were to follow, holding on to the planks or to some broken pieces of the ship. And this was how we all got safely ashore.

In Malta

28 When we were safely ashore, we learned that the island was called Malta. ²The natives there were very friendly to us. It had started to rain and was cold, so they built a fire and made us all welcome. ³Paul gathered up a bundle of sticks and was putting them on the fire when a snake came out, on account of the heat, and fastened itself to his hand. ⁴The natives saw the snake hanging on Paul's hand and said to one another, "This man must be a murderer, but Fate will not let him live, even though he escaped from the sea." ⁵But Paul shook the snake off into the fire without being harmed at all. ⁶They were waiting for him to swell up or suddenly fall down dead. But after waiting for a long time and not seeing anything unusual happening to him, they changed their minds and said, "He is a god!"

⁷Not far from that place were some fields that belonged to Publius, the chief of the island. He welcomed us kindly and for three days we were his guests. ⁸Publius' father was in bed, sick with fever and dysentery. Paul went into his room, prayed, placed his hands on him, and healed him. ⁹When this happened, all the other sick people on the island came and were healed. ¹⁰They gave us many gifts, and when we sailed they put on board what we needed for the voyage.

From Malta to Rome

¹¹After three months we sailed away on a ship from Alexandria, called "The Twin Gods," which had spent the winter in the island. ¹²We arrived in the city of Syracuse and stayed there for three days. ¹³From there we sailed on and arrived in the city of Rhegium. The next day a wind began to blow from the south, and in two days we came to the town of Puteoli. ¹⁴We found some believers there who asked us to stay with them a week. And so we came to Rome. ¹⁵The brothers in Rome heard about us and came as far as Market of Appius and Three Inns to meet us. When Paul saw them, he thanked God and took courage.

In Rome

¹⁶When we arrived in Rome, Paul was allowed to live by himself with a soldier guarding him.

¹⁷After three days Paul called the local Jewish leaders to a meeting. When they gathered, he said to them, "My brothers! Even though I did nothing against our people or the customs that we received from our ancestors, I was made a prisoner in Jerusalem and handed over to the Romans. ¹⁸They questioned me and wanted to release me, because they found that I had done nothing for which I deserved to die. ¹⁹But when the Jews opposed this, I was forced to appeal to the Emperor, even though I had no accusation to make against my own people. ²⁰That is why I asked to see you and talk with you; because I have this chain on me for the sake of him for whom the people of Israel hope."

²¹They said to him, "We have not received any letters from Judea about you, nor have any of our brothers come from there with any news, or to say anything bad about you. ²²But we would like to hear your ideas, because we know that everywhere people speak against this party that you belong to."

²³So they set a date with Paul, and a larger number of them came that day to where Paul was staying. From morning till night he explained and gave them his message about the Kingdom of God. He tried to convince them about Jesus by quoting from the Law of Moses and the writings of the prophets. ²⁴Some of them were convinced by his words, but others would not believe. ²⁵So they left, disagreeing among themselves, after Paul had said this one thing, "How well the Holy Spirit spoke through the prophet Isaiah to your ancestors! ²⁶For he said,

'Go and say to this people:
You will listen and listen, but not understand;
    you will look and look, but not see.
²⁷ Because this people's minds are dull,
    they have stopped up their ears,
    and have closed their eyes.
Otherwise, their eyes would see,

their ears would hear,
their minds would understand,
and they would turn to me, says God,
and I would heal them.'"

²⁸And Paul concluded, "You are to know, then, that God's message of salvation has been sent to the Gentiles. They will listen!" [²⁹After Paul said this, the Jews left, arguing violently among themselves.]

³⁰For two years Paul lived there in a place he rented for himself, and welcomed all who came to see him. ³¹He preached about the Kingdom of God and taught about the Lord Jesus Christ, speaking with all boldness and freedom.

INDEX

The main subjects in the Introduction are listed, excluding Church, God, Good News, Jesus, Paul and Peter

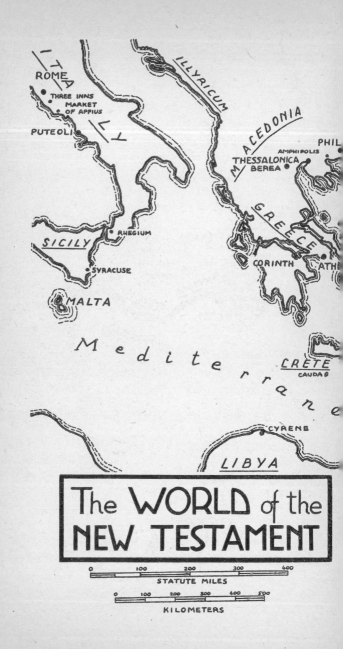

ITALY

ROME
THREE INNS
MARKET
OF APPIUS
PUTEOLI

ILLYRICUM

MACEDONIA
AMPHIPOLIS
THESSALONICA
BEREA
PHIL

SICILY

RHEGIUM

SYRACUSE

MALTA

GREECE

CORINTH

ATH

Mediterrane

CRETE
CAUDA

CYRENE

LIBYA

The WORLD of the NEW TESTAMENT

0   100   200   300   400
STATUTE MILES

0   100   200   300   400   500
KILOMETERS

THE BIBLE READING FELLOWSHIP

Readers of this commentary may wish to follow a regular pattern of Bible reading, designed to cover the Bible roughly on the basis of a book a month. Suitable Notes (send for details) with helpful exposition and prayers are provided by the Bible Reading Fellowship three times a year (January to April, May to August, September to December), and are available from:

UK
The Bible Reading Fellowship,
St Michael's House,
2 Elizabeth Street,
London SW1W 9RQ.

USA
The Bible Reading Fellowship,
P.O. Box, 299, Winter Park,
Florida 32789,
USA.

AUSTRALIA
The Bible Reading Fellowship,
Jamieson House,
Constitution Avenue,
Reid,
Canberra, ACT 2601,
Australia.